Customized Books

Customized books for your school, organization, or business are available for larger quantity orders. Please contact the author at kberntzen@katherineberntzen.com.

Feedback

I would appreciate your feedback upon reading this book. I invite you to take my survey at www.katherineberntzen.com/survey.pdf.

Facebook and Twitter

I hope you will find helpful and useful information on my Facebook and Twitter pages. For access to these sites, please go to www.katherineberntzen.com.

IN PURSUIT OF MY SUCCESS™ FOR TEENS

Developing a College, Career, and Money Plan for Life

Second Edition

Dedication

To Petter, love of my life and best friend

To my nieces and nephews, Will, Kellie, Matts, Ida, Mari, Jon, Even, and Emma, may

you live happy and fulfilling lives

IN PURSUIT OF MY SUCCESS™

FOR TEENS

Developing a College, Career, and Money Plan for Life

Second Edition

Katherine Berntzen

Published by Katherine Berntzen, Inc.
Katherine Berntzen, Inc.
P.O. Box 478
Naperville, IL 60566

Please visit the author's website, www.katherineberntzen.com.

In Pursuit of My Success™ is a trademark claimed by Katherine Berntzen and may not be used without the prior written permission of Katherine Berntzen.

Paperback: ISBN-13: 978-0-9823452-3-8, ISBN-10: 0-9823452-3-2

Subject Matter: Teen Inspiration, Self-Help, College Planning, Career Planning, Financial Literacy, Personal Finance, Financial Planning, Budget Management

Contents

Acknowledgments

Thank you to Petter for his unconditional support. Thanks to many friends, family, clients and others through the years who inspired my thoughts for this book. Thank you to Shannon Walker, a foreclosure and bankruptcy expert, for her financial insight.

Preface

Recently I have been thinking about my life and wondering what I should have known early on, before going to college and before going to work full-time. This book is for those of you who want to learn a few simple things before starting out on your own. If you learn and apply to your life a few of the tips from this book, you will be several steps ahead of everyone else. Of particular importance is the chapter on "Money for College, Money for Life." The chapter on "Money for College, Money for Life" will give you life skills you must have, that is, if you want to feel more secure.

The focus of this book is to help you develop a College, Career, and Money Plan, and to help you understand some of the behaviors necessary for success now and in the future.

May you develop a plan, define how you want to behave, achieve your goals, and be successful in *your* own eyes.

Part I

What is the College, Career, and Money Plan?

The College, Career, and Money Plan is a planning tool designed for high school students. The College, Career, and Money Plan will help you, the high school student, begin planning your college education, your career, and your financial future. This book provides a backbone for understanding what recruiters and employers are looking for and translates it into what you can do for yourself to select a college, select a career, make better life decisions including financial decisions, and be more visible to employers.

How to Benefit the Most from This Book

At the end of this book, you will be asked to develop a College, Career, and Money Plan. I would suggest reading through this entire book first to generate thoughts and ideas before attempting to complete the College, Career, and Money Plan worksheet. The College, Career, and Money Plan you develop will become a map for your future and will allow you to set goals for yourself. I recommend re-evaluating and making changes to your plan at least once per semester or quarter throughout high school and college. After you begin your career, review and update your College, Career, and Money Plan once each year to reflect what you actually did the previous year, new priorities in life, new opportunities, and new thoughts. The additional tools and concepts presented in this book can be referenced throughout your lifetime.

Why Write This Book

I want you to have a college education, a sustainable and fulfilling career, a stable financial future, and to be physically and mentally healthy. Studies show these factors are related to each other. If you are well educated, have a job you love and work with people you like, are paid well, are good with your money, are surrounded by positive friends who support you, then you are more likely to be both physically and mentally healthy. Life is filled with choices, and my goal is to help you understand the bigger picture so that you can make better decisions for yourself throughout your lifetime.

Everyone has the choice, whether you want to believe it or not, to go to college and earn an associate's degree, bachelor's degree, master's degree, PhD, MD, law degree or other degree. Why would you even want to earn a higher degree? There are two reasons. First, the unemployment rate is lower for those with higher degrees.[1] This means, you have a greater chance of being employed if you have a higher degree. Second, average salaries are higher for those with higher degrees.[1] The higher the education level you achieve, your chances of earning a higher income are greatly improved.

According to the U.S. Census Bureau, in 2009, the average income for persons 25 years of age and over with less than a high school diploma or GED was $24,289 per year.[2] For those with a high school degree, the average annual income was $32,812.[2] For those with some college, the average income was $38,612.[2] For those with an Associate's degree, a planned two year degree, the average annual income was $41,529.[2] A Bachelor's degree, a four year degree, yielded $58,762 in average annual income, and a Master's degree, typically a two year degree following a Bachelor's degree, yielded $74,217 in average annual income.[2] A Professional degree, such as a medical or law degree yielded $128,578 and a Doctoral degree, such as a PhD, yielded $103,353 in annual income.[2] Keep in mind, these incomes are averages which include less experienced workers and very experienced workers. You will make a lot less money with less work experience, for example, at age 25, than with more work experience at age 40.

To put these income levels into perspective, the U.S. Census Bureau reports the poverty threshold in the United States in 2009 was $11,161 for one person under the age of 65, $14,366 for two adults under the age of 65, and $21,756 for two adults and two children in a household.[3] Now compare these poverty thresholds to the average incomes above. Now I hope you will understand why I want you to go to college and create opportunities for yourself.

I encourage you to read on and discover what you can do for yourself today and in the future, no matter who you are or where you come from. Reading this book is your chance not only to be on even ground but to be several steps ahead of everyone else. While I cannot promise you will achieve all of your goals, because there are so many factors involved including those we cannot control, I can promise by reading this book and completing the College, Career, and Money Plan, you will be better prepared for life than you would have been. I hope this book will help you get started planning for your future.

How This Book Was Written

I wrote this book with the hope it would interest you, through presenting my personal stories and providing possible scenarios that are true to life. Repetition is used throughout the book to help make it easier to learn new concepts and terms, which you need to know throughout your lifetime. At times, I encourage you to keep reading when difficult information is presented, because again, repetition is used and additional examples will be provided. The footnotes, tables, and websites are excellent references for you to use in your search for answers. Overall, I hope I will convince you to do something good for yourself and others, today and through the years, each time you consult this book.

Part II

Introduction to the College, Career, and Money Plan

First, and foremost, you must figure out what you want to do for a living, and then select your major and degree(s) to be earned. Do not be discouraged if you do not know exactly what you want to do for a living at this stage in your life. This book will help you get there.

When I was in high school, I was very shy and somewhat sheltered about what the real world had to offer. I had no real clue what I wanted to do for a living and did not have exposure to different types of careers. I went to college because it was expected of me, although my family and I never analytically discussed what my career might be, as is the case with most families. It never occurred to me I would not go to college, but it also never occurred to me I needed to firm-up my career aspirations and plan my college degree around my career. I never made the connection. I looked at a major and said "What can I do with a degree in Spanish or Economics or Political Science?" However, I should have said, "I want to be a management consultant and advise companies on improving operations. What degree(s) should I earn to do this?" I was lucky I found my passion in my early 30's. However, I would like for you, the reader, to find your passion much sooner than I did.

When we are in our teens, many of us do not know exactly what we want to do for a living. We have a few dreams or ideas but nothing is firmed-up in our heads. You should know, that is okay. This book will help you develop a College, Career, and Money Plan for as many careers as you are considering. Seeing optional career plans will help you to eliminate careers you no longer want to consider, and sharpen your thoughts on which career you will target. So as not to waste time and money, you should decide what career you want and what your degree(s) will be

BEFORE you have completed 45 semester hours in college, approximately one and one-half years. Your first year in college will be filled with taking basic courses such as English, History, and Mathematics. Ideally, but not always realistically, you should decide on a career before you enter college.

If you already know what you want to do for a living after you graduate from college, congratulations because you are a step ahead of everyone else. However, keep reading, because I can almost guarantee you will find some tips you most likely have not seen or heard before.

Determine Your Interests

To help you start thinking about what you would like to do for a career, you should determine your interests.

What type of tasks have people repeatedly said you are good at doing, whether at school, work, or home. Examples of tasks include: organizing, speaking to groups, speaking a foreign language, writing, tutoring or teaching, planning parties, fund raising, writing software programs, re-building engines, fact-finding, wiring systems, carpentry, knowing interesting facts about the universe, identifying plants, identifying dog breeds, or sharing medical facts.

What type of behaviors have people you care about told you they admire about you. Are you organized, diplomatic, a leader, empathetic, cooperative, strong-willed? These are just examples.

What subjects do you like in school, what extracurricular activities do you enjoy (i.e. Debate Team, Latin Club, Science Club, Yearbook Committee, Community Service), and what do you enjoy most when you have time off from school (i.e. reading current events, writing papers or articles, analyzing statistics, reading about scientific discoveries, understanding how electronics work, understanding how engines work, helping people, identifying plants or animals, identifying marine life, hiking, star gazing, playing soccer, boating, building structures, learning geography and cultures, learning languages, writing software programs, designing inventions, writing scripts and producing films). Ask yourself why you enjoy these activities. Are there any activities or interests you have not yet pursued but would like to pursue? I will share some of my own examples to help you start thinking.

Looking back in time, people told me I was good at planning and organizing, advising, and fact-finding. As far as behaviors go, people told me I was mature-minded, helpful, tactful, respectful, and tenacious. The subjects I liked in school were Math, Chemistry, English, Spanish, and Physical Education. I liked Math, because I could do it, usually. I liked Chemistry for the same reason. I typically scored well on English exams. I took Spanish from the third grade through when I was a Senior in high school, as I enjoyed exposure to another culture through language and foods. I enjoyed physical education, because I liked surprising people that the "skinny" girl could run, jump, play volleyball, do more chin-ups than any girl or boy, and dodge the ball in "dodge ball" faster than anyone. I see this as the competitive side of me and the side of me that always looks for a better way to do something. You will know what I mean by this when you read on.

In high school, I was Vice President and then President of the Spanish Club. What I enjoyed about the Spanish Club was further exposure to a foreign language and culture through competitions and trips. I also enjoyed the camaraderie and leadership experience. Even though I was very shy, I still wanted to be a leader. Being President of the Spanish Club forced me to try on my leadership hat and to speak in front of a group, which was very hard for me at the time. It was a terrific experience, and I am glad I did it.

I was a member of the Girl Scouts from sixth grade through 12th grade. We had the same troop members, plus or minus a few, and the same leaders through all those years. We were lucky. What I enjoyed about the Girl Scouts was learning new tasks to which I had not been previously exposed and helping others in the community. I also enjoyed the camaraderie, leadership, travel, downhill skiing, and nature experiences.

Translate Your Interests into a Field or Industry of Interest

Now given your interests from above, can you translate your interests into a specific field or industry in which you might want to work? If you are not quite sure which field interests you yet, then explore some options by researching various fields and industries in your school, college, or public library, or on the internet. Is it News Media, Healthcare, Manufacturing, Construction, Architecture, Astronomy, Teaching, Economics, French, Geology, Genetics, Human Resources, Insurance, Law, Fundraising, Charity Organizations, Sales, Marketing, Information Technology, Accounting, Finance, or the Coast Guard? Ask yourself why you want to work in this field. What is interesting about it? Does it match your interests from above? You may decide at this point you are interested in several fields, and that is okay. Some people will only be interested in one field. Some people will always be interested in multiple fields. However, at some point and most likely BEFORE you have completed 45 semester hours in college as mentioned previously, you will have to select one field, and perhaps a back-up field, in which to pursue a career. Consider the possibility that other fields of interest could be pursued as a hobby. For example, my interest in languages, geography, and cultures has translated to a hobby in U.S. and world travel, an expensive hobby nonetheless. I have also continued my interest in helping others through volunteerism.

In talking with many people, I found our interests do not change very much over time. Our interests may evolve as we build our skill sets and are exposed to new fields, but the primary interest is still there. For example, I have always had an interest in making improvements. When I was in high school, I held a job at a bank where I implemented a new filing system. This was before sophisticated computer systems. In college, I held a job where I suggested and redesigned a message pad to save time. I took a lot of messages! I also assisted in the implementation of my employer's first asset management program, keeping track of computers and word processing equipment. In my first job out of college, I took the initiative to streamline a recruiting process for which I administered. I wanted to save time. I also took the initiative to start a large organizational networking group to help improve business results through personal and professional development. I have always been looking for a solution for improving effectiveness and efficiency even when it comes to my own work. I could never be satisfied with the status quo. That is just who I am. I have not changed over time, but as I have been exposed to more complex projects and been exposed to new industries, my skill set has increased, and I now perform more complex tasks. You could say I translated my interest in effectiveness and efficiency to the field of management consulting.

Values

What are your values? What is important to you when it comes to a work environment and culture? Do you want to work with supportive, very smart people who challenge you to be your best? Do you like working in a team? Do you want to be left alone while working but trusted to get the job done correctly? Do you want to work in an office or in a non-office setting or both? Do you want to work around a lot of outgoing people, or do you want to work in quiet surroundings, or does it matter? Would you like to go to the same office each and every day, or would you like to travel or both? Keep in mind if you travel 100% of the time, you will have a very limited personal life. Do you want to work only from 8:00 A.M. to 5:00 P.M., Monday through Friday? If this is the case, you may limit your career choices and your earning potential. However, I have to say I know very effective managers who consistently deliver planned business results, work mostly from 8:00 A.M. to 5:00 P.M., and have been promoted through the years. I believe this is because the company culture is in alignment with the managers' values. There will be more on this in the chapter on "Selecting an Employer Right for You."

Limitations

Do you have any limitations that would prevent you from pursuing your field of interest? Hopefully the answer to this question is "no." Most of us will not have any limitations other than what we tell ourselves. If someone has told you that you have limitations, think twice about the motivations of that person.

Ideal and Ultimate Job

Now ask yourself, what would be your ideal and ultimate job? If you could do any job in the world within the field or industry you identified above, what would it be and is it in alignment with your interests and values? At this point, you may have identified several possible ideal and ultimate jobs. Using my above example, I translated my interest in effectiveness and efficiency to the field of management consulting while utilizing my skills in advising, fact-finding, and organization. My ideal and ultimate job is one as a management consultant, providing operational performance improvement services to clients in various industries. As far as my values go, I do not like going to the same office each and every day of the year. I like varied work. I like change. I like seeing results. I enjoy working with people who are different from me, which makes my life and work more interesting. I am a workaholic. I am organized. I am creative.

Another way to look at it is what do you want to do at the height of your career, say your fifth or sixth job after college? At the height of your career do you want to be a Software Consultant, Financial Analyst, Accountant, President and CEO of a manufacturing company, solid and trustworthy Mechanical Engineer, Director of Engineering, Ethicist, Tenured Professor, Teacher, Management Consultant, Journalist, Law Partner, Corporate Attorney, Family Practitioner, Orthopedic Surgeon, Geneticist, Physician Assistant, Nurse, Nurse Manager, Dietitian, Epidemiologist, Public Health Educator, Director of Customer Service, Supply Chain Director, Plant Manager, Vice President of Operations, Executive Director of a non-profit organization, Geologist, well-respected Economist, solid Market Research Analyst, Salesperson, Sales Manager, Director of Sales, Vice President of Sales, solid and trustworthy Investment Analyst, Money Manager, Stock Market Analyst, Vice President of Investments, or successful Artist? You are not limited to this list.

At this point, you may decide to explore some options by researching careers in your school, college, or public library, or on the internet. Remember, everyone will have different interests and values. Once you have some ideas about fields of interest and specific jobs within those fields, talk with people in those fields to gain a better understanding of what they do. Please be sure to read the entire book first, including the chapter on "Networking" before attempting to do this. You might perhaps work during the summer in high school and college in a field you find interesting and prove to yourself you enjoy it or you do not. The bottom line is you will be working to support yourself and perhaps a family for 40 years or more, after you graduate from college, and you must select a career you enjoy. You should know, some people work in the same career field throughout their lifetimes, and other people choose to have several different careers throughout their lifetimes, due to life experiences, work experiences, and new opportunities. We are always changing and growing.

Career Paths

After you have identified an ideal and ultimate job, then the next step is to identify possible career paths leading up to your ideal and ultimate job. (In most cases, there will be more than one career path, and you should also know the career path varies by company. However, the point of this exercise is to develop a plan and to be aware of different career paths for future reference. Your goal is to achieve your ideal and ultimate job.) In other words, what position title or responsibility level would be appropriate for a first "real job" after college, second job, third job, fourth job, fifth job, sixth job, and so forth that would lead up to your ideal and ultimate job. The sequence of jobs leading up to your ideal and ultimate job is the career path. Each job on a career path should show increasing levels of responsibility and be related to your ideal and ultimate job on some level. One example of a career path in Human Resources (HR), and there are many paths depending on the company, would be: HR Specialist, HR Manager, HR Director, and HR Vice President. In this example, HR Specialist is the first job after college, and HR Vice President is the ideal and ultimate job.

The job title is a short label, describing the job and responsibility level. Refer to **Table 1** for an outline of general responsibility levels by title and a generic organization chart. The titles are intended as a guideline only and will apply to many larger for-profit companies and some not-for-profit organizations. Of course, specific responsibility levels are determined by individual companies. Keep in mind, organizations are more complex than depicted in **Table 1**, as there may be more management levels, but this is a great way to see how a simple organization within a company might look.

How long does an employer expect someone to serve in each job on the career path? You may expect to be in each job on the career path from one to four or more years, and each job should match your interests and values as previously discussed. Again, the goal is for each job on the career path to have increasing levels of responsibility and to be related on some level to your ideal and ultimate job. A prospective employer wants to see increasing levels of responsibility on a resume.

Each job on the career path will have specific job entry requirements such as degree(s), certification(s), and job skills. In other words, you must have earned specific degrees, perhaps certifications, gained specific job experience, and learned specific job skills to be considered for a particular job. Job skills may include leadership, communication, analytical abilities, problem solving abilities, financial skills, negotiation skills, public speaking, and many more. Of course, the job skills required vary, depending on the job and the employer, but it is up to you to find out or to determine what the general job entry requirements are, regardless of employer, and to use those general job entry requirements as goals to achieve in order to get the job you want. Importantly, once you learn general job entry requirements for each job on your career path, you must analyze if you are willing to work hard and build your skills throughout your career to obtain your ideal and ultimate job. If not, you will need to revisit your ideal and ultimate job.

Once you have identified the career path, job title, and responsibility level for each position on the career path, and general job entry requirements, you will need to learn how much in salary, in general terms, each position on the career path will earn.

The chapter on "Networking" explains how you can learn specific career path information for your ideal and ultimate job.

Earning Priorities

These next questions are mind-boggling for anyone of any age, but I am going to ask you to think about these questions now, because it can be important when finally selecting a career.

Table 1

General levels of responsibility for many larger for-profit and some not-for-profit organizations

- In general and for simplicity reasons, an entry level position such as a Specialist, Analyst, or Associate will have no one reporting to the position, and this role will be a contributor to a company objective or overall goal. This person may work in a team or work individually. Whatever position title and responsibility level you select, and it varies from company to company, be sure before you accept a position with a company that the position is promotable. A promotable position is one in which a person serving in the position can be promoted to a management position within a company. Some company cultures separate management positions from administrative/technical positions. If the position is classified as an administrative/technical position, most likely the position will not be promotable. However, the only way to be sure is to ask before you accept the position. You should be sure to ask the hiring manager *and* to ask the Recruiter at the very least. If either one of them tells you "no" the position is not promotable, then the position most likely is not promotable. A Specialist, Analyst, or Associate most likely will report to a Manager.
- A Manager may or may not have anyone reporting directly to the position and the level of responsibility may or may not impact company profits or customer satisfaction. However, a Manager should have greater responsibilities and more complex responsibilities than a Specialist, Analyst, or Associate. A Manager may report to a Director.
- A Director may have a department of people within a particular speciality area, such as Human Resources or Marketing or Purchasing or Information Technology or Manufacturing or Hospital Emergency Department, reporting directly to the position and the level of responsibility most likely will impact company profits and/or customer satisfaction and/or employee satisfaction. A Director may report to a Vice President.
- A Vice President may manage multiple departments, territories and perhaps multiple specialty areas, depending on the company, and the level of responsibility most likely will impact company profits, customer satisfaction and employee satisfaction. A Vice President may report to a CEO.
- A Chief Executive Officer (CEO) has responsibility for an entire company.

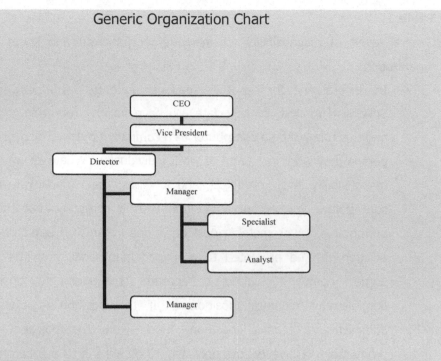

Generic Organization Chart

The above organization chart implies three possible career paths:

- Analyst, Manager, Director, Vice President, CEO

- Specialist, Manager, Director, Vice President, CEO

- Manager, Director, Vice President, CEO

What are your earning priorities? In other words, how much money do you need to earn in order to support yourself with the basics and luxuries in life? The best way to answer this question is to start with how much will it cost you to live when you turn 25, 30, 35, 40, 45, 50, 55, 60 and 65? Consider the cost of renting an apartment, buying a home, buying a car, car insurance, renter's or homeowner's insurance, homeowner's assessment fees, health insurance, medical bills not covered under health insurance, electricity, gas, water, trash service, phone, cell phone, cable, high speed internet access, and the list goes on. What are your student loan payments? How much will it cost to buy food, entertainment, clothes, cleansers, toiletries, furniture, and other items and services? Consider the cost of having children and pets. How much will you have to spend on annual home maintenance, such as painting inside or outside, landscaping, replacing a roof, or replacing windows? How much will you owe in property taxes each year? If desired, what will it cost to take an annual vacation? How much money do you need to save for retirement and when do you want to retire, if at all? How much in assets (i.e. cash, real estate, investment accounts, retirement accounts) do you want to have when you reach 25, 30, 35, 40, 45, 50, 55, 60, and 65 years of age? How much money do you need to save each year in order to achieve your goals?

When considering how much it costs to live, keep in mind, the cost of living in different parts of the country. Sometimes salaries are higher in high cost areas but not always. You have to do your research to find out. See **Table 2** for Salary Information by City. When you go to the referenced websites in **Table 2**, you will see two terms used: median and mean. The term, median, is the point at which half the data in the study is above the median, and half the data in the study is below the median. The term, mean, is another word for average. Using the two terms "median" and "mean" simply allows us to compare numbers. That's all. You will need to get used to these two terms as you will see these terms in college textbooks and throughout your lifetime. While this sounds complicated, I encourage you to keep reading.

If you would like to live in the Chicago area, the median price of a home in 2009 was $199,200.[4] If you would like to live near the beach in the Corpus Christi, Texas area, the median price of a home was $134,300 in 2009.[4] If you decide to live in the Portland, Oregon area, the median price of a home was $244,100 in 2009.[4] As you can see, the price of a home varies by city. See **Table 3** for a sampling of median home sales prices. The term "median" means half the homes are priced above the median, and half the homes are priced below the median. Specifically, if $493,300 is the median sales price of a home in the San Francisco area, half the home sales prices were above $493,300 and half the home sales prices were below $493,300. Using the term "median" in this way allows us to compare cost.

Table 2

Salary Information by City
These websites provide *free* salary information by city for specific job titles and type of jobs: www.salary.com   www.bls.gov/oes/current/oessrcma.htm

Now consider how much money in salary do you need to earn in order to accomplish your goals at 25, 30, 35, 40, 45, 50, 55, 60 and 65? From your total salary, you will need to deduct the cost of social security, Medicare, Medicaid, and local, state, and federal income taxes. This is your "take home pay" or net salary. Is your "take home pay" enough to accomplish all of your goals?

Table 3

2009 Metropolitan Area - Median Home Sales Prices[4]

San Francisco, CA	$493,300
New York, NY	$381.400
Portland, OR	$244,100
Miami, FL	$211,200
Chicago, IL	$199,200
Birmingham, AL	$146,100
Corpus Christi, TX	$134,300
Florence, SC	$114,500
Indianapolis, IN	$114,200
Grand Rapids, MI	$87,400

By learning what it costs to live based on your personal needs and wants, by finding out how much money you can earn in each position on your chosen career path as we discovered in the previous section, you can begin to understand your earning priorities. The chapter on "Money for College, Money for Life," the chapter on "Networking," and the College, Career, and Money Plan worksheet at the end of this book will help you organize your thoughts.

Ideal and Ultimate Job Revisited

At this point, you should revisit your ideal and ultimate job and the chosen career path to determine if it is a good fit for you. Will each job on your chosen career path provide you with enough money to support your basic needs such as food and shelter, pay for student loans, car loans, and other needs and wants? Please be sure to read the chapter on "Money for College, Money for Life" before answering this question. Are you willing to work hard to achieve your ideal and ultimate job? If you answered "no" to either of these two questions, you will need to revisit your ideal and ultimate job. Remember, you are selecting a career that is right for you and will help you achieve your personal and professional goals.

Select a Major and Degrees to be Earned

Select a major and degrees to be earned related to your ideal and ultimate job(s). In other words, what major and degree(s) do you have to select in order to obtain the positions on your career path? If you decide you want to be an attorney, you may decide to obtain a BA or BS in Economics or Liberal Arts, as many attorneys do, before entering law school. If you want to be a doctor, you may decide to obtain a BS in Zoology or BS in Biology before entering medical school. If you want to be a chemical engineer, you may decide to obtain a BS in Chemical Engineering. If you want to be a Human Resource Analyst/Manager/Director/Vice President, you may decide to obtain a BA in Human Resource Management or BS in Management and an MA in Organizational Psychology or Master of Organization Behavior. (The type of degree varies by college.) If you decide you want to be a Public Health Educator, you may decide to obtain a BS in Biology or BS in Nursing and an MPH in Public Health Education. There are so many options. Remember, which career you choose should be based on your interests and your values -- not what your best friend decides to do. Selecting a career based on what your best friend decides to do, can be a recipe for disaster, because while you may respect your friend, you are two different people with different sets of interests, values, experiences, and skills.

Finding Answers

Before researching and developing your answers, I would recommend reading this entire book, as this book will provide you with more background and detail.

There are some excellent career and salary websites. The Bureau of Labor Statistics offers an outstanding website for finding careers based on your interests and also includes general salary information, www.bls.gov/k12/index.htm. Use this website to start thinking about what type of career might be of interest to you. Don't limit yourself to the careers provided. As an exercise, brainstorm with friends, family, teachers, and counselors, to suggest similar, yet different, careers. Next, try using Americas Career InfoNet, www.careerinfonet.org or the Bureau of Labor Statistics' Occupational Outlook Handbook, www.bls.gov/oco, to gather more ideas about careers based on your interests. Both of these websites provide general salary information, as well. See **Table 4,** Career and Salary Information. For gathering *free* salary information based on job title or type of job and city, try www.salary.com and www.bls.gov/oes/current/oessrcma.htm. See **Table 2**, Salary Information by City.

Once you discover potential career fields or industries that are in alignment with your interests, try googling these fields and industries. Read as much as you can until you decide it sounds interesting or not. Googling job titles, perhaps using generic titles from **Table 1**, in specific fields and industries can also be very informative. Job titles will usually return job ads with application (entry) requirements and job descriptions. For example, try googling Human Resources Analyst, Human Resources Manager, Human Resources Director, Vice President of Human Resources. Notice the level of responsibility, job skills required, experience required, and education required for each position. Then instead of Human Resources, insert the field or industry of interest to you plus the title (Specialist, Manager, Director, Vice President). You will learn job titles and job descriptions are different from company to company. Use your creativity to learn as much as you can about a field, industry, and specific jobs.

Table 4

Career and Salary Information

- The Bureau of Labor Statistics has an outstanding website on finding careers based on your interests. This website provides salary information as well. www.bls.gov/k12/index.htm.
- Americas Career InfoNet provides helpful career, degree, and salary information. The latest web addresses are: www.careerinfonet.org or http://acinet.org.
- Learn about careers in the following fields: the Arts, Teaching, Engineering, Law, Social Services, Life and Physical Sciences and many more from the Bureau of Labor Statistics' Occupational Outlook Handbook: www.bls.gov/oco/.

In addition to written resources, you should be sure to talk with people who hold careers of interest to you in order to sharpen your thoughts on a career and career path. Ask your parents, teachers, and trustworthy adults you know from after-school activities and in your neighborhood as approved in advance by your parents, to help you identify people in these careers to talk with you so that you can learn more about the work and decide if it is in alignment with your (desired) skills, values, and interests. Be sure to conduct your written research first before talking in depth with people about their own careers, as you do not want to waste their time or your time on something you may not be interested in. The chapter on "Networking" will be helpful in guiding you through the process of talking with people about careers.

Money for College, Money for Life

This chapter is one of the most important chapters in the book, as having money is important to our physical and mental well-being. Because we all have different backgrounds and education, you may not fully understand the concepts of this chapter upon reading it the first time. I encourage you to read and re-read this chapter until you understand it. You will get it. You have to get it, because you have to be good with money.

Everyone has to have money to buy the basics in life, such as food, shelter, and clothing. If you want more than the basics in life you will have to work hard to earn money and to save money. You must convince yourself you *will* be good with money, because you *have* to be good with money – even if your parents are not. With respect to money, life is not about how much money you have, but it is about being able to live in peace without living from paycheck to paycheck. If you know someone who has done this, you know what I mean. Living from paycheck to paycheck is a vicious cycle that is difficult to get out of, and it can haunt you each and every day, because you worry if you can make next month's payments and what will happen if you cannot make the payments. Being good with money is your chance to be a step ahead of everyone else and to live in peace.

When I was in college I made very little money and lived from paycheck to paycheck. I always worried about money and if I would have enough money for food and rent. It still haunts me to this day, and I believe that is why I have chosen to be good with money.

Plan How You Will Pay for College

When you are a Freshman and not later than when you are a Junior in high school, I would recommend you investigate the colleges of your choice and understand the tuition, fees, cost of books, and living expenses involved for obtaining the degree(s) you are considering. You should not expect your parents to pay for your college education. Paying for your entire education would be very nice but is not always realistic given the high cost of tuition. Keep in mind, your parents may receive reduced social security payments from the government upon retirement age, and perhaps reduced retirement pensions, if any. The performance of their retirement accounts and other investments are dependent on the state of the economy. As a result, it is important to be cognizant of what your parents can and cannot afford without putting them at risk for financial disaster.

You need to have a conversation with your parents right away about what they are willing to commit to your education and living expenses, if anything. Then plan accordingly.

If your parents are willing to fund or help fund your college education, be sure to ask them at least twice each year when you are in high school if they still will be able to contribute. When you are in college, continue to ask each semester or quarter until you graduate from college. That way, there are no surprises, and *you* have control over *your* future.

If your parents say they are going to pay for some or all of your college education, ask your parents *how* they are going to pay for your college education, to help them start thinking about it, if they have not already. To help fund your college education, your parents may have participated in one of the two 529 Plans (also known as Qualified Tuition Programs) available, which includes a pre-paid tuition program and a college savings plan[5]; Coverdell Education Savings Account[6]; or Education Savings Bonds[7]. You can read about each of these plans in the Reference section located in the back of this book. Also, your parents may benefit from cash back credit cards, providing they pay-off their balance, the amount due, each month. If they have to finance their credit card purchases, then the benefit is gone completely, and the finance charges will set them back. I will talk about credit cards later. If your parents have not invested in a plan, they may be planning to pay for your education using other methods. These methods might include: sell off their own assets (things they own such as real estate or mutual funds), obtain a home equity loan (not recommended for any purpose as they could lose their home if they fail to make payments), obtain a student loan for you, use their own savings, work a second or third job, or other creative method.

If your parents are unable to commit to helping you pay for college, then you should plan to pay for college yourself.

If it is your responsibility to pay for your college education, either in whole or in part, and this is the case with many of us, you need to develop a plan for how you will pay your share. Your options include obtaining student loans, earning scholarships and grants, and work-study programs. Additional options include co-op programs and internships, offered by employers, as well as other part-time and full-time employment, which may be advertised by the College Career Center of the college you select or through employer websites. Please see the chapter on College Career Centers. Some students will use a combination of these options to pay for college.

Federal Government Financial Aid for Student Loans, Scholarships and Grants, and Work-Study Programs. You should review these websites when deciding how you would like to fund your college education, whether you are interested in student loans (paid either by you or your parents), scholarships and grants, and work-study programs: www.college.gov, www.ed.gov, www.studentaid.ed.gov, and www.federalstudentaid.ed.gov, and www.fafsa.gov. Each of these websites is controlled by the U.S. Department of Education. Each site ends in ".gov" which means it is a government website. A website ending in ".com" is a commercial website and is NOT a government website. You will see there is an overlap of information on these websites, which can be confusing. However, some websites provide unique information, and it is important to read each website. After you have perused the above sites, I recommend reading the latest edition of the publication, *Funding Education Beyond High School: The Guide to Federal Student Aid* by the U.S. Department of Education which can be found at www.studentaid.ed.gov/pubs. You can also google it, but make sure it is the latest edition. This document is *free* and provides the most comprehensive information including eligibility requirements, protecting yourself from identify theft when applying, scholarships, grants, work-study programs, loans (for both parents and students), government service awards, loan forgiveness, incentives for the military, and much more. All of the buzzwords you have heard about are discussed in this document: Pell Grant, TEACH Grant, Iraq and Afghanistan Service Grant, Federal Supplemental Educational Opportunity Grant (FSEOG), Federal Perkins Loan, William

D. Ford Direct Loans, Direct Stafford Loans, Direct PLUS Loans, and Direct Consolidation Loans. It's all in this document.

When you are ready to apply for *Federal* and some *State* student loans, grants, and work-study programs, go to www.fafsa.gov. Because the website *ends* in ".gov" you know it is a government website, and this is where you want to go. FAFSA stands for *Free* Application for Federal Student Aid. To be clear, you apply for federal loans, grants, and work-study programs on one application, and the application is located at www.fafsa.gov. FAFSA is a U.S. Department of Education administered program. You should know *a majority of all student loans are provided by the U.S. Department of Education.* The www.fafsa.gov website allows you to complete an online application *or* complete a PDF format application, which you snail mail to the government. Before you complete an application, you need to do three things.

1) Application Deadline. Learn application deadlines for both Federal aid and State aid, and these deadlines are located on the www.fafsa.gov website. I would recommend applying for aid as soon as you can, as funds may dry up if you wait until mid-term or the deadline to apply.

2) Eligibility Requirements. Learn if you are eligible to receive any aid by using the FAFSA calculator at www.fafsa.gov, and you can also read about eligibility requirements at www.ed.gov/fund/grants-college.html, www.studentaid.ed.gov/completefafsa, and the publication from above, *Funding Education Beyond High School: The Guide to Federal Student Aid.*

3) Review the Application Form Instructions. Go to the PDF format application, located on the www.fafsa.gov website, and review the instructions before you complete the form to determine which documents you need to apply. Additional instructions for completing the FAFSA form are located at www.studentaid.ed.gov/completefafsa. Additional help can be found in *Funding Education Beyond High School: The Guide to Federal Student Aid.*

Additional Financial Aid. Financial aid may be available through the colleges you are considering as well as state governments.

The Financial Aid Office of the colleges you are considering should be helpful in answering questions about the FAFSA and should let you know about any specific loans, grants, or work-study programs that are specific to the college. Make sure when applying for financial aid through FAFSA, that you specify on the application which colleges you would like to receive your financial aid application eligibility results.

You might be able to apply for financial aid through the state or state's higher education agency in the state where your selected colleges are located.

Regardless of where you get your help, be sure to keep track of deadlines, and apply at the earliest time possible, as funds can dry-up early.

Private Loans. You may also inquire about the cost of student loans at the bank where your family has its checking and savings accounts as well as any established, reputable, neighborhood banks. You can find banks in your area by going to www.fdic.gov. FDIC (Federal Deposit Insurance Corporation) regulates the financial services industry. As with any loans, I would not respond to phone, mail, e-mail, internet ads, yard signs, signs posted to bulletin boards, visits to your home, or other solicitations for loans, as these may be scams even though the names used may be legitimate banks. Sometimes "banks" you have never heard about may also contact you. I would expect student loan scams to increase as the cost of tuition increases. Remember, this is your life, and it is important you have a good start. To read about specific scams targeting college students, review the publications under "Consumer Protection" at www.studentaid.ed.gov/pubs. For general information about protecting you, the consumer, please refer to **Table 1**, Consumer Protection.

Loan Costs. I would avoid taking a student loan, if at all possible, because you will have to pay the money back with interest, and having to do so will set you behind financially until you pay-off the loan. However, if taking a loan is your only option, by all means, you must do it so you can achieve your goals, but make sure you can afford to pay back your student loans based on the expected salary from your first job. I encourage you to keep reading, as this book will show you how to determine if you will be able to afford student loans, if any, based on your expected salary.

Before taking out a student loan, or any loan for that matter, it is important to shop for a loan that will cost you the least amount of money over the life of the loan. You should consider closing costs and fees associated with closing on your loan as well as any penalties and other fees above and beyond the interest rate. (From the bank's perspective, the loan sale is "closed" at the time you sign the contract.) You will need to understand if the interest rate is fixed or adjustable (i.e. variable, changing) and if the rate is compounded annually or more frequently. Again, what you are concerned about is the *overall* cost of the loan, how much you will have to pay in closing costs and associated fees, interest, and other fees over the life of the loan. A fixed interest rate means the interest rate will be the same each and every year during the life of the loan. An adjustable (i.e. variable, changing) interest rate means the interest rate you pay is tied to a key financial indicator in the market beyond your control, such as the prime rate, and the interest rate you pay could increase or decrease over time, depending on your loan terms. Most likely the interest rate will increase, which will increase the amount of your monthly payments when you start paying back your student loans. Adjustable interest rates may be offered at lower interest rates compared to fixed interest rates initially, but your future payments will be unknown. Taking an adjustable interest rate loan is risky and could bankrupt you in the future. The only time I can think of when it is less risky to take out a variable interest rate loan is when interest rates are high, say 14%, and interest rates are expected by a majority of financial industry analysts to decrease over the *life of your loan*. However, this does not happen very often. I would avoid taking an adjustable interest rate loan if you can.

Keep in mind, for a student loan, or any loan such as a mortgage for a house, you can always re-finance, when you find a lower and better interest rate from a reputable financial institution; however, you need a good credit history to do this. You will learn more about establishing credit later in this chapter. When you re-finance, it means you take out a new loan with the same financial institution or a different financial institution, and this new loan should pay-off the old loan.

If you have taken out a number of student loans, government or private, you can consolidate by re-financing those loans into one loan to simplify your payments; however, you still need to be concerned about the overall cost of the loan. If you reduce your monthly payments by extending the life of the loan or loan period, then this costs you more money. I know that by running the numbers, which you will be able to do later, based on your learnings from this chapter.

Loan Contract. When exploring student loans, or any loan for that matter, it is important to understand the lender's requirements, such as closing costs, all fees, fixed or adjustable interest rates, the date you must begin paying back the loan, and importantly, you should consider your own needs.

Once you have decided where to get your student loan, based on your cost comparison study, whether it is through the U.S. Department of Education by applying at www.fafsa.gov or your local bank, be sure to read and understand the entire loan contract *before* you sign it, and make sure the information is accurate based on what you were told by the lender. You can develop your own spreadsheet to confirm the bank's interest, fees, and monthly payment calculations are accurate. Be sure to ask questions before signing the contract about anything you do not understand in the contract. Asking questions is a part of your financial education and managing your life. Any lender that would respond to questions in an abrupt or condescending manner is not professional, and I would not do business with that lender. I would recommend hiring an attorney to ensure the contract is honorable.

With respect to student loans, you need to understand by when you should apply for your loan to ensure you will receive the money in time to pay tuition, as required by your college. Very importantly, you need to understand when the first payment is due to the bank. The first payment due date tells you by when you must have a job, so you can make your student loan payments.

Please note, all of the fees and closing costs, for any loan, should be stated clearly within the contractual documents. Before you sign the contract, you should know exactly how much it is going to cost you in fees and closing costs to take out the loan. The fees and closing costs on the contract should be the same or less than the fees and closing costs the lender quoted to you. If not, seek a different lender. Review again your loan cost comparison study from above to understand if the fees and closing costs, of the bank you selected to get the loan from, are in alignment with reputable banks. If not, seek a different lender. The reason I say this is that a few lenders have charged outrageous fees and closing costs, in the thousands of dollars, way above what is standard for the industry. Do not let this happen to you.

In general, the loan contract should identify the loan terms (requirements), such as fees to be paid and under what circumstances, identify the interest rate as "fixed" or "adjustable," identify when the first payment is due and when the last payment is due, also known as the loan period. If the loan has a fixed interest rate, the contract should specify what the specific interest rate is (i.e. 5%) throughout the life of the loan. If the loan has an adjustable, or changing, interest rate, the contract should specify what key financial indicator the interest rate is tied to (i.e. prime rate), how many percentage points above the financial indicator you will be charged (the margin), how often the rate can increase, the maximum percentage increase allowed each time the rate increases, and the interest rate ceiling. The interest rate ceiling is the highest interest rate that can be charged to you during the life of the loan. You need to make sure there is *not* a fee for paying off your student loan, or any loan, early. A loan contract is a legally binding contract, and you should consult an attorney to review the contract for you to ensure it is honorable. If the lender is in a hurry and does not allow you time, such as several weeks, to review the contract, then there is something wrong, and you should seek a different lender. You will need to ask if you can lock-in to an interest rate, as interest rates go up and down depending on the market, while you review the contract, but do NOT sign the loan contract until you have fully reviewed and approved the loan contract. If you take out a loan and decide later you do not like the contract terms, it is too late. You must pay back the loan according to the terms in the contract. That is why you must be very careful before signing any contract. It is always okay to insert your own clarifications into a contract. You and the lender should initial and date each addition or change in a contract and each page of the contract. Further, you should keep a copy of each and every page of the contract after you and the lender have signed and dated it, and keep it in your records for a lifetime. See **Table 1** for information about the Consumer Financial Protection Bureau.

Other Sources of Scholarships. There are other sources of scholarships, including private scholarships offered by corporations, foundations, other non-profit organizations, in addition to state government entities and the colleges to which you are applying. Be aware of application deadlines which can occur as early as the summer before your Senior year.

To learn about private scholarships and grants for undergraduate and graduate school, go to www.studentaid.ed.gov/scholarship, which allows you to search for some private scholarships. Also, I recommend asking your school counselor or librarian for books with a listing of private scholarship opportunities for which you can apply. The books should be current year publications in order to obtain the most updated information with respect to application requirements and deadlines. You can also find these books in any bookstore. Once you have identified some sources, you will want to go to the websites of the specific organizations to confirm requirements, confirm deadlines, and complete an application.

I recommend reviewing scholarship information during your Freshman year and not later than your Junior year, so you can begin to understand what scholarship providers are looking for. The purpose is to allow you to set goals for yourself, such as taking specific classes required by a scholarship provider or achieving a certain Grade Point Average. Planning ahead is to your advantage.

The state's higher education agency in the state where you plan to go to college may offer scholarships. You can learn about these scholarships on their websites or through the financial aid office, of the colleges you are considering. Again, the college's financial aid office may have information for you regarding other scholarships.

Table 1

Consumer Protection

Consumer Financial Protection Bureau. The Consumer Financial Protection Bureau (CFPB) was created in 2010 by Congress. The central function of the CFPB is to protect consumers from financial companies. The CFPB does this by educating consumers and monitoring full transparency of costs passed on to you when taking out any loans, including student loans and mortgages, credit cards, and other financial products and services. You can sign up for the latest updates on the CFPB website at www.consumerfinance.gov. You can also submit your complaints to the CFPB.

Federal Trade Commission. The Federal Trade Commission (FTC) is a federal government entity that enacts laws and policies designed to protect you, the consumer. The FTC provides free information on its website, www.ftc.gov, concerning a number of issues including identity theft, free credit reports, bankruptcy, scams, and outright fraud. In 2006, $1.2 billion was reported as stolen through fraudulent activities. Consumers were robbed of their money through a number of methods: 45% e-mail, 16% mail, 15% internet websites, 13% phone, and 10% other. Be sure to check the FTC's website to learn all you can about protecting yourself, the consumer, and visit the website often to learn of current scams. The FTC recommends checking your credit report at least once per year, and this can be done free of charge through the FTC's website, www.ftc.gov/freereports.

Attorneys General. Each state has an Attorney General who is responsible for protecting businesses and consumers from illegal activity, including fraud. Consumers can file complaints with the Attorney General's office in the appropriate state. To find the Attorney General website in your state, you can google "Attorney General" and then the name of your state such as, "Texas." For example in Texas, the web address is www.oag.state.tx.us. In New York, the web address is www.ag.ny.gov. In California, the web address is www.oag.ca.gov. I recommend reviewing the Attorney General website for your state from time to time to learn about the latest scams so that you can protect yourself and your family.

Legal Services Corporation. Legal Services Corporation (LSC), also known as Legal Aid, is a government entity providing free legal services to low-income persons for matters ranging from consequences of not paying back student loans to rental disputes to scams. LSC provides an even better picture of the types of scams that are out there and provides free online brochures for what you can do to protect yourself, before anything happens. To find the website for your state, go to www.lsc.gov/map/index.php. This is a great website for anyone, including college students who are out on their own for the first time.

Many scholarships do not pay for your entire college education but can help you with some of the cost. Today, if I knew my college education was going to cost me $80,000, I would apply for at least $80,000, probably a lot more, in scholarship money, and/or apply for full scholarships with a number of schools, with the hope I would receive a scholarship award. Writing a few simple scholarship applications and essays is much easier than working two or more jobs over a long period of time, and it will be easier on your wallet if you do not have to obtain student loans.

The most important thing to keep in mind is that not all scholarships are the same. Some scholarships are not based on financial need or academics, and of course, some are. Some scholarships are so specific they require you to live in a specific fraternity house, to study biology, or to study piano. If nothing else encourages you to read scholarship books, you can read these books for the entertainment factor. In fact, hold a contest with your friends to find the most specific, unique, or amazing scholarship, while you are searching for suitable ones for yourself!

To show the variety of scholarships, below are two noteworthy scholarships.

- The Utah System of Higher Education offers the New Century Scholarship, which requires a student to earn an Associate's degree by the time the student graduates from a Utah high school or to complete a special math and science curriculum. The student must also meet GPA and ACT requirements. The student may go to any Utah System of Higher Education institution including BYU and Westminster. Please go to www.higheredutah.org/scholarship_info for more information.

- The International Council of Shopping Centers (ICSC) Foundation offers scholarships to both undergraduate and graduate students. One scholarship, the Schurgin Family Scholarship, awards a $5000 scholarship to an undergraduate Junior or Senior who is pursuing a real estate or similar degree and wants to work in real estate development, retail real estate, or shopping center leasing. Through the Undergraduate Real Estate Award, the ICSC offers 25 - $1000 scholarships, which are awarded based on recommendations from the dean of selected schools and programs. The website provides a phone number to call to inquire about participating schools. Please go to www.icsc.org/foundation for more information.

Working. If you will be working through college, know you are not alone. According to the Bureau of Labor Statistics, in October 2009, about 51% of full-time and part-time college students worked or were looking for work.[8] Forty seven percent (47%) of full time college students and eighty five (85%) of part time college students worked or were looking for work.[8] Congratulations if this is the route you are taking. It is very difficult to work while going to college, but it can be done! As you will see later in this book, having work experience in your chosen field will be to your advantage when looking for a real job after graduation.

Taxes

If your parents will not be financially supporting you through college, your parents will have to understand they can no longer claim you as a dependent on their federal, state and local income tax statements that are filed each year. Your parents should not receive the tax benefit of you as a dependent if they are not supporting you. Regardless, if you have work income or other income including scholarships or grants, you will have to file your own federal, state, and local income tax forms. You can learn more about what is federally taxable on the Internal Revenue Service website, www.irs.gov under "Taxable Income for Students," and you can calculate an estimate of your federal income taxes from the latest "1040EZ Form" using the "1040EZ Instructions," downloadable from the IRS's website. I would advise reviewing this website when planning how to pay for college, as you need to ensure you will have enough money to pay your tuition, fees, books, rent and other living expenses, after paying taxes. In addition to federal income taxes, you may need to file state and local income taxes. To get the instructions and forms for estimating and filing state and local income taxes, you can google "1040 Form" or "1040EZ Form" plus your taxable state, such as Ohio, and locality, such as Cincinnati. See **Table 2**, Income Taxes.

Disposable Income

You will hear the term *disposable income* throughout your lifetime. Disposable income is money that can be used for savings and expenses, *after* paying federal income taxes, state income taxes, FICA, property taxes, and other personal

Table 2

Income Taxes

Federal Income Taxes. The agency responsible for collecting income taxes at the federal level is the Internal Revenue Service. You can learn about "Taxable Income for Students" and estimate federal taxes to be paid by using the latest "1040EZ Form" and "1040EZ Instructions," located on the IRS website, www.irs.gov.

State Income Taxes. Most states have a state income tax. To learn if your state has an income tax, go to the "Department of Revenue" or "Department of Taxation" website for your state or simply call the phone number in your phone book. The same form, 1040, would need to be filed if your state taxes income. (1040EZ is a shortened version of the 1040 and may or may not be offered in your state.) It is important to make sure the website is an official government website, and the website will most likely have an ending such as ".gov" or ".state.hi.us" for Hawaii or ".state.md.us" for Maryland. I would not read tax information provided on a website that is not a government entity, as the information could be wrong, consequently getting you into trouble.

Local Income Taxes. Some localities, such as cities, have an income tax. To learn if your locality has an income tax and which form to file, you can either look up the phone number in the phonebook and call to ask, or you can try to find the official government website. The catch is to figure out the name of the agency. The agency might be called Income Tax Bureau, Income Tax Department, Department of Revenue, Department of Taxation or a variation. Another option is to go to the main website for the locality.

Please note: You will *never* be asked to enter your social security number or other private information on these websites. If you are asked this information, then you are on a fraudulent website. Conversely, if you call to ask for general information, no one should ask you for your social security number.

taxes such as license taxes.[9,10] (Please note: The definition of disposable income varies, depending on the study. Therefore, when reviewing disposable income data in a study, it is important to read the study's definition of disposable income. However, in general, we can say disposable income is income after taxes are paid.) To repeat, disposable income is what you have left, after paying taxes. There are two things you can do with your money after paying taxes: save it or spend it.

Most likely you will hear about disposable income on the news and in conversations with people when talking about the state of the economy. Everyone, educated or not, talks about the economy, because the state of the economy impacts them. The economy impacts your parents. The economy impacts you. For example, you might read oil prices consume .7% or 1% of disposable income in the economy, or whatever the concern is at the time. You can be sure if economists are reporting this information to news organizations, it impacts you eventually. The price of oil impacts just about everything, because we need "fuel" to power manufacturing activities, distribution centers, office buildings, homes, apartments, cars, and trucks for distribution of products to be sold at your favorite store. We also use oil in various products, such as for making plastic and carpet. When governments and businesses spend more money on "fuel," they may have to cut spending in other areas, such as the number of employees, office supplies, etc., because, like us, they only have so much money they can spend. We, consumers, business, and government, form the economy. We are all the economy. That is why the government keeps track of economic numbers such as disposable income. You can read about disposable income and other economic indicators from the U.S. Department of Commerce's Bureau of Economic Analysis at www.bea.gov.

What does disposable income mean to you? Disposable income can be calculated in the aggregate (as a whole) for the economy as well as for individuals. You can calculate your own disposable income. As an exercise, I encourage you to calculate the percent of your disposable *personal* income used at the gas pump in one week. If you are not working, then select a number less than $500, which is realistic for a part-time job. You can learn how to calculate percentages in **Table 3**. If you make $100 per week, after paying taxes, in a part time job, and gas for your car costs you $50 per week, that means, gas pump prices gobble up 50% of your disposable personal income. Ouch! As another example, if you make $100 per week, after paying taxes, in a part time job and gas costs you $30 per week, gas gobbles up 30% of your disposable personal income. (We assume you drive the same distance and realize the same gas mileage in both examples.) In this second example, you would have $20 more per week to save or spend on other things, compared to the first example. This is just one of so many different comparisons you can do with disposable Income.

If we spend more money this year on fuel than we did last year, and our income is the same both years, then we will have less money to save and spend on other things. You can see it in the above example and in your own numbers. That

my math.) Please see **Table 3**, Calculating Percentages. Some of this money will go toward the down payment on a home loan and car loan, will buy nice furniture, electronics, appliances, a new roof, a new driveway, or anything else you need. The rest of the money will be saved for retirement. These lifetime savings figures do *not* include any interest income or investment income.

What are interest income and investment income? In simplistic terms, interest income is income that is earned through placing your money in an interest bearing account such as a money market account, savings account, or a certificate of deposit. For example, if you place $12,000 in an interest bearing money market account which yields an annual interest rate of 4%, then the annual interest income is $480 ($12,000 x .04 interest = $480). Please see **Table 4**, Calculating Interest Income.

Investment income includes gains achieved through investments such as stocks, bonds, mutual funds, and real estate. If you purchase land today for $12,000 and sell it for $18,000 five years from today, your investment earnings or gain over the five year period would be $4,500 ($18,000 - $12,000 - $1500 in property taxes paid for all five years = $4,500), and your percentage gain over the entire five year period would be 38% ($4,500 gain / $12,000 original purchase price = .38 x 100% = 38%). If you calculate the percentage gain in terms of how much you earned each year, this annualized gain would be 7.6% (38% / 5 years = 7.6%).

Table 3

Calculating Percentages

One of the most useful mathematical tools I ever learned was how to calculate percentages. Everyone should know how to do this in their head for simpler calculations, by calculator, and on a computer spreadsheet such as Excel. I calculate percentages almost every day of the year, whether I am at work or on vacation. Why would I do such a thing? I use percentages to calculate server tips in a restaurant (10% of the total check if the service was fine and 20% if the service was outstanding), interest rates on savings accounts (interest I expect to receive), interest rates on loans (interest I expect to pay to financial institutions), the percentage of my salary I can save each month for retirement (for planning purposes), the percentage of my salary I can save each month until I have saved enough money to put 20% down on a home, calculating what a 20% down payment would be on a $150,000 home I want to purchase, and many more. Calculating percentages is easy, and everyone can do it and should do it as it is a first step for becoming financially savvy.

Example 1

I dined in a restaurant and my total bill was $25.00. Service was okay and therefore I chose to leave a 10% tip. 10% multiplier = 10 / 100 = .10. To calculate the tip amount, I take $25.00 x .10 = $2.50. To calculate it in my head, I simply move the decimal over to the left by one space. This is always the case for 10%.

Example 2

My restaurant bill was $25.00. Service was exceptional and therefore I chose to leave a 20% tip. 20% multiplier = 20 / 100 = .20. To calculate the tip amount, I take $25.00 x .20 = $5.00. To calculate it in my head, and the easiest way for me to do it, I calculate 10% tip first ($2.50) and then add an additional 10% ($2.50). 10% + 10% = 20% ($2.50 + $2.50 = $5.00).

Example 3

My restaurant bill was $25.00. Service was pretty good and therefore I chose to leave a 15% tip. 15% multiplier = 15 / 100 = .15. To calculate the tip amount, I take $25.00 x .15 = $3.75. To calculate it in my head, I calculate the 10% first, then I calculate the 5%. 10% + 5% = 15%. To calculate the 10% tip, I move the decimal over one space to the left, $2.50. To calculate the 5% tip, I know that 5% + 5% equals 10%. 10% of $25.00 is $2.50. Therefore half of $2.50 is $1.25. $1.25 is 5%. Finally, I add 10% or $2.50 + 5% or $1.25 = $3.75. $3.75 is 15% of $25.00.

Example 4

My grandfather gave me $1000 in January. I decided to put this money in a two year certificate of deposit (CD) at my family's neighborhood bank which offered the highest interest rate and no fees, other than for early withdrawal, which I do not expect to have to do. The guaranteed interest rate is 5% per year and the interest is compounded (calculated and then added to the present value of the CD) annually. (I know that compounding more frequently, such as monthly or even better daily, will increase my total interest earned, but compounding annually was the best deal I could find at this time.)

At first, I decide I want to know how much in interest I can earn in a one year period. 5% / 100% = .05. $1000 x .05 = $50. The interest I would earn in a one year period is $50.

I realize I can calculate the total value of my CD at the end of the one year period by taking ($1000 x 1) + ($1000 x .05) = $1050. A shortened form of the same calculation is $1000 x 1.05 = $1050. The value of my CD at the end of one year is $1050.

Then, I decide I want to know the total value of my CD at the end of the two year period. Since the CD is compounded (calculated and then added to the present value) annually, I know at the end of the first year, my CD is worth $1050, from above. To calculate the interest earned at the end of the second year only, I take the value at the end of the first year times the interest multiplier, $1050 x .05 = $52.50. The interest earned for the second year only is $52.50. To calculate the total interest earned in both the first and second years, I take $50 + $52.50 = $102.50. To calculate the total value of my CD at the end of the two year period, I take $1000 + $102.50 = $1102.50 *or* $1050 x 1.05 = $1102.50.

You will see another formula for calculating compound interest in **Table 4**, Calculating Interest Income.

Example 5

I plan to save for a down payment on a home. I would like to buy a $150,000 home in a five year period. To avoid paying monthly mortgage insurance premiums, I decide to put down 20%. When I say" put down 20%," that means I plan to save 20% of the value of a $150,000 home that I would hope to find in five years. 20% multiplier = 20 / 100 = .20. $150,000 x .20 = $30,000. To calculate this number in my head, I know 10% + 10% = 20%. To arrive at 10% of $150,000, move the decimal one place to the left, which equals $15,000. 10% or $15,000 + 10% or $15,000 = $30,000. $30,000 is 20% of $150,000.

Now I know my specific goal is to save $30,000 in a five year period. If I save in equal amounts each year, I will have to save $30,000 / 5 years = $6000. I will have to save $6000 each year over the five year period to achieve my goal of saving $30,000. I currently earn $50,000 in salary. The percentage of my income I will have to save each year is $6000 / $50,000 = .12 *and* .12 x 100 = 12%. If I make $50,000, and I save $6000 per year, I will have to save 12% of my salary each year.

Table 4

Calculating Interest Income

Interest income is income you earn on your money when it is placed in an interest bearing account such as a checking account, money market account, savings account, or a certificate of deposit. Most accounts earn interest, but not all accounts earn interest. You need to do your due diligence (research) when comparing accounts at institutions. You need to compare interest rates and any fees. Be careful with fees, because the fees could wipe away any interest benefit.

The two formulas below can be used to calculate interest, compounded monthly or annually. You would use these calculations when you want to estimate how much money you would have in the future, based on the amount in the account at a specific point in time. You can also confirm the amount of interest paid to you by the bank is accurate.

The term compounded means the number of times interest is paid or is to be paid to your account. Therefore, you ideally want to be paid interest as often as possible in order to make more money on the account, given the same interest rate. Two percent (2%) interest paid *monthly* is better than 2% interest paid *annually*. You will see this in the below examples.

Again, why would you want to calculate interest? You would want to calculate interest for two reasons:

1) To determine how much interest you will earn for planning purposes.

2) To confirm the interest paid to you by the financial institution is accurate.

When you see the formulas, don't get distracted by what they look like. These are actually easy formulas you can use throughout your lifetime. Remember to start working the parenthesis from the inside to the outside, and you will do just fine. It takes practice to get it right, and I know you can do it.

These calculations apply to both fixed and adjustable (variable or changing) interest rates. If the interest rate is adjustable, you can only calculate the current interest rate that you know. When the interest rate changes, re-do the calculations.

At the end of this table, I will show you the Excel formulas. Compare your answers computed by calculator with your answers computed by Excel.

Compounded Monthly

If you want to calculate the ending balance of your account after interest is added to the original amount in the account at a point in time, use this formula:

$$P \times [1 + (i / 12 \text{ months})]^{n \text{ in months}} = T$$

If you want to calculate interest earned or to be earned, use this formula:

$$P \times [[1 + (i / 12 \text{ months})]^{n \text{ in months}} - 1] = I$$

or

$$T - P = I$$

Compounded Annually

If you want to calculate the ending balance of the account after interest is added to the original amount in the account at a point in time, use this formula:

$$P \times (1 + i)^{n \text{ in years}} = T$$

If you want to calculate interest earned or to be earned, use this formula:

$$P \times [[(1 + i)^{n \text{ in years}} - 1]] = T$$

Or

$$T - P = I$$

i = Interest rate expressed as a decimal

n = Deposit Term. The expected or actual number of months or years in the account

P = Principal = Amount in the account in $ at a point in time

T = Total ending balance (value) of the account in $ after interest is added to the Principal at the end of the term. This is the same as Principal + Interest = T

I = Interest earned or to be earned in $ (Does NOT include Principal)

Example 1

I plan to deposit $500 in a savings account. I did my research and found Bank A offered the best fixed interest rate at 2%, *compounded monthly*. I want to know how much my money will be worth in one year, one and one-half years, and two years, if I do not add any more money to my account.

I use the Compounded Monthly formula:

One Year = **12** Months

$P \times [1 + (i / 12 \text{ months})]^{n \text{ in months}} = T$

$\$500 \times [1 + (.02 / 12 \text{ months})]^{12} = \$510.09 = T$

$P \times [[1 + (i / 12 \text{ months})]^{n \text{ in months}} - 1] = I$

$\$500 \times [[1 + (.02 / 12 \text{ months})]^{12} - 1] = \$10.09 = I$

or

$T - P = I$

$\$510.09 - \$500 = \$10.09 = I$

At the end of one year, I have earned \$10.09 in interest. At the end of one year, my account balance (value) is \$510.09.

One Year and 6 Months = 12 Months + 6 Months = **18** Months

$P \times [1 + (i / 12 \text{ months})]^{n \text{ in months}} = T$

$\$500 \times [1 + (.02 / 12 \text{ months})]^{18} = \$515.21 = T$

$P \times [[1 + (i / 12 \text{ months})]^{n \text{ in months}} - 1] = I$

$\$500 \times [[1 + (.02 / 12 \text{ months})]^{18} - 1] = \$15.21 = I$

or

$T - P = I$

$\$515.21 - \$500 = \$15.21 = I$

At the end of one and one-half years, I have earned \$15.21 in interest. At the end of one and one-half years, my account balance (value) is \$515.21.

Two Years = **24** Months

$P \times [1 + (i / 12 \text{ months})]^{n \text{ in months}} = T$

$\$500 \times [1 + (.02 / 12 \text{ months})]^{24} = \$520.38 = T$

$P \times [[1 + (i / 12 \text{ months})]^{n \text{ in months}} - 1] = I$

$\$500 \times [[1 + (.02 / 12 \text{ months})^{24} - 1] = \$20.38 = I$

or

T – P = I

$520.38 - $500 = $20.38 = I

At the end of two years, I have earned $20.38 in interest. At the end of two years, my account balance (value) is $520.38.

What if I decide to add money to my account every month? How do I calculate that? I simply add the new amount I deposited in my account to the T. This becomes my new P.

For example, I decide to add $50 to my savings account each month. I still earn 2%, compounded monthly. I want to know how much my account will be worth each month. I need to know this in order for my own financial planning purposes and to make sure the financial institution is calculating the interest correctly. I will compare my own calculations with my bank statement each month.

Month 1

$$P \times [1 + (i / 12 \text{ months})]^{n \text{ in months}} = T$$

$$\$500 \times [1 + (.02 / 12 \text{ months})]^{1} = \$500.83$$

At the end of Month 1, I add $50 to my account.

$50 + $500.83 = $550.83

Month 2

$$P \times [1 + (i / 12 \text{ months})]^{n \text{ in months}} = T$$

$$\$550.83 \times [1 + (.02 / 12 \text{ months})]^{1} = \$551.75$$

At the end of Month 2, I add $50 to my account.

$50 + $551.75 = $601.75

Month 3

$$P \times [1 + (i / 12 \text{ months})]^{n \text{ in months}} = T$$

$$\$601.75 \times [1 + (.02 / 12 \text{ months})]^{1} = \$602.75$$

At the end of Month 3, I add $50 to my account.

$50 + $602.75 = $652.75

Month 4

$$P \times [1 + (i \ / 12 \text{ months})]^{n \text{ in months}} = T$$

$$\$652.75 \times [1 + (.02 \ / 12 \text{ months})]^{1} = \$653.83$$

I have $653.83 at the end of Month 4.

You can continue this exercise for an entire year.

Example 2

I plan to deposit $500 in a savings account. Bank B offered me a 2% fixed interest rate, *compounded annually*. I want to know how much my money will be worth in one year, one and one-half years, and two years, if I do not add any more money to my account.

One Year

$$P \times (1 + i)^{n \text{ in years}} = T$$

$$\$500 \times (1 + .02)^{1} = \$510.00 = T$$

One and one-half years = 1 year + 6months/12months =

1 year + 6/12 = 1 year + .5 year = **1.5** years

(I can do this because 12 months = 1 year.)

$$P \times (1 + i)^{n \text{ in years}} = T$$

$$\$500 \times (1 + .02)^{1.5} = \$515.07 = T$$

Two Years

$$P \times (1 + i)^{n \text{ in years}} = T$$

$$\$500 \times (1 + .02)^{2} = \$520.20$$

Analysis: Bank A in Example 1 offers a better interest rate, because the interest is compounded monthly. I will make more money with Bank A's 2% interest rate compounded *monthly*, than I will with Bank B's 2% interest rate compounded *annually*. While this does not make a big difference with a small amount of money in the bank, it is money that is owed to me, and it is money I can save for the future. Over time, this money adds up.

Example 3

I am now 40 years old, and I will deposit $200,000 in a certificate of deposit (CD) at my local bank. The CD term is 2 years, and the interest rate is fixed at 3% per year. A CD is a type of account offered by financial institutions which may pay higher interest rates than a savings account or money market account. Unlike a savings account or money market account, you cannot withdraw any of your money from the CD until the end of the contracted term without penalty. In this example, the term is 2 years. CDs can be 3 months, 6 months, 1 year, 2 years, or really any period of time as offered by the financial institution. Before investing in a CD, make sure you do not need your money for the entire CD term.

$$P \times (1 + i)^{n \text{ in years}} = T$$
$$\$200,000 \times (1 + .03)^2 = \$212,180$$

$$T - P = I$$
$$\$212,180 - \$200,000 = \$12,180$$

The interest paid to you is $12,180

NOTE:

You should be aware when shopping for the best interest rate for checking, savings, money market, or Certificate of Deposit, financial institutions will quote an interest rate, fixed or variable, and an APY (Annual Percentage Yield). Financial institutions should provide you with both rates, and if they do not, ask. The APY is another way of looking at interest, whether it is fixed or adjustable (variable, changing). The APY is a bank's calculation based on the advertised, current interest rate and considers planned rate changes, such as tiered and stepped interest rates. When shopping for the best deal that will bring me the most amount of money, I start by comparing the APY, but it doesn't stop there. I also compare the interest rate, as the interest rate is what I use when planning for the future, along with any fees and charges. I want to limit charges to my account and make the most amount of money overall. The APY is a calculation you can find on FDIC's website, www.fdic.gov, in the document *Annual Percentage Yield Calculation*. FDIC regulates how financial institutions can calculate the APY.

Excel Formulas

Below are formulas you can use in Excel in order to calculate *fixed* and *adjustable* interest rates. If the interest rate is adjustable (variable, changing), it means the rate could go up or down, based on a key financial indicator in the market of which you have no control. Each time the interest rate changes, you can compute the new interest earned or to be earned for the appropriate time period using the new rate. **The steps to follow include: 1)** Enter the information in Column A **2)** Enter the information in Column C **3)** Enter the formulas in B8, B10, B20, and B22 exactly as is **4)** Finally, enter the known numbers in B4, B5, B6, B16, B17, and B18.

I recommend setting up the formulas and then making sure you get the correct answers based on the Examples in this table. Always double check and triple check the formulas to ensure accuracy, before running any numbers.

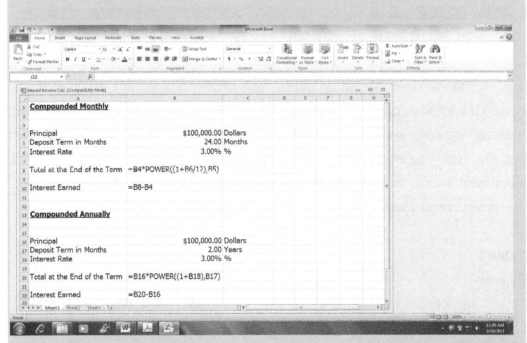

After entering the known numbers in **Step 4**, the answers will appear where the formulas were entered.

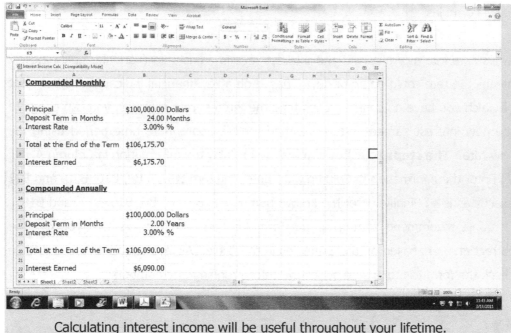

Calculating interest income will be useful throughout your lifetime.

You will need interest and investment income in order to keep up with and exceed the inflation rate, which has been around 2% - 5% per year. Inflation is the "general" increase in the price of goods (products) and services, such as groceries and car repair services. Again, you want the percentage of your interest and investment income to be much more than the inflation rate. See **Table 5**, Inflation *and* Inflation and Taxes.

Table 5

Inflation
Inflation is the "general" increase in the price of goods (products) and services per year. Inflation has been around 2% - 5% per year. As an example of an increase in the price of goods (products) and services, consider a restaurant visit today may cost $12 per person, but one year from now at a 3% inflation rate, the cost at the same restaurant for the same food may cost $12.36 ($12 x .03 or 3% inflation rate = $.36 inflation (+ $12) = $12.36).
Also consider any savings you have in a bank. Your goal should be to earn interest far greater than the inflation rate, and you want the highest possible interest rate, which can be found through shopping banking institutions. If the inflation rate is 3% per year, and your money market account or savings account or bank certificate of deposit earns 2% interest per year, you have lost 1% of the value of

your money (2% - 3% = - 1%) due to inflation, the rising cost of goods and services in the marketplace.

In summary, buying the same goods and services you bought this year will cost 3% more next year if the inflation rate is 3%. Therefore you will need to earn 3% more in income next year so you can buy the same goods and services next year. You want your income, whether it is savings interest income or your salary, to be much greater than the current and expected future inflation rate. The higher the savings interest rate, the better, because this means more money in your pocket for future use.

Inflation and Taxes

Now consider inflation and taxes when calculating how much minimum interest you need to earn on a money market account or savings account or bank certificate of deposit in order to break even, not lose money. If you make $40,000 in salary and have $12,000 in a money market account that earned 4% annual interest, making your interest earned for the year at $480, under current tax laws for Illinois, just to pick a state, your approximate federal and state effective tax rate on $40,480 is 14%. The effective tax rate is your total amount paid in federal, state, and local income taxes divided by your total gross income, that is, income before paying taxes. I know this by completing the Federal and Illinois 1040EZ Forms. Your total income tax obligation on $480 is $67.20 ($480 x .14 = $67.20). The actual earnings on your investment is $412.80 ($480 - $67.20 = $412.80). That makes your actual interest earnings on your investment at 3.44% and not 4% ($412.80 / $12,000 = .0344 x 100 = 3.44% vs. $480 / $12,000 = .04 x 100 = 4.00%). Note the interest reduction for taxes paid is .56% (4% interest – 3.44% = .56%). As you can see, if the inflation rate is 3% and you are taxed at the 14% effective rate, then you are ahead by only .44%. If you calculated the interest income at .44% over a 30 year period, the amount would be very small, too small.

The latest U.S. inflation rate, information about inflation, and the CPI Calculator can be found through the U.S. Department of Labor, Bureau of Labor Statistics, Consumer Price Index at www.bls.gov/cpi. The CPI Calculator is a fun way to see the value of your money over time.

Interestingly, you will earn less in interest on say, a money market account, when you have less money. For example, a bank may offer a money market interest rate of 1% per year for having a minimum balance of $1000, and the same bank may offer a money market interest rate of 2% per year for having a minimum balance of $100,000.

Ten percent (10%) as an overall annual percentage of investment gains, such as on stocks and mutual funds, is oftentimes a goal cited by financial advisers, but this goal is less commonly achieved. I would certainly have a goal of 10% return per year on my investment but know that my actual return might be around 6% or 7% or less in a given year. While you want to earn the most on your money, your investment, you do not want to fool yourself into believing you will have more money in the future than you actually will. See **Table 6**, What is the Stock Market? *and* Savings Account vs. Stock Market.

Building on the previous example, if you saved 10% of your salary each year over a 45 year period and received a 6% gain each year, then in 45 years your money would be worth $1,171,460, excluding inflation. If you saved 8% of your income each year over a 45 year period, and received a 6% gain each year, your

Table 6

What is the Stock Market?
Public companies raise money to run their businesses through issuing and selling stock to the public (you and me) and institutions (companies and government entities). This stock is sold on a stock market exchange such as the New York Stock Exchange. However, the public goes to a brokerage firm, such as Charles Schwab, to purchase stock. When you purchase stock, you are investing your money. Each public company is assigned a stock symbol as recognized by the Securities and Exchange Commission (SEC), www.sec.gov. The stock symbol is an easy way of identifying which stock you purchased. The SEC is a government entity, responsible for overseeing the securities industry, including protecting investors, you and me.
The public and institutions also purchase mutual funds. Mutual funds are groups of individual company stocks lumped into one fund, and each mutual fund has its own symbol as recognized by the SEC. Each mutual fund has a fund manager who is responsible for buying and selling stocks within the fund and ultimately, the performance of the fund.
In general terms, the public and institutions buy stocks and mutual funds with the hope the price will increase over time. When the price has increased sufficiently for the investor, the stock or mutual fund can be sold at a profit. Stocks

and mutual funds are usually held for a period of time, such as one to five years or more.

It can be beneficial to buy stocks and mutual funds that pay dividends. Dividends are an extra "bonus" paid on each stock share, usually quarterly, to owners of stock (shareholders). How much the company pays in dividends to its owners of stock (shareholders) depends on how well the company does financially. Only some stocks and mutual funds pay dividends, and dividends are not guaranteed. With that said, it is a good idea to find companies that have a history of paying dividends. The higher the dividends paid, the better. Keep in mind, you still want the stock price to increase over time.

Savings Account vs. Stock Market

You will need to save money for now and for the future.

When you are younger and in need of money for cars, homes, furniture, and the basics in life, I would advise keeping this money in a high interest money market account or savings account.

Investing in the stock market is advantageous when you have been purchasing stocks and mutual funds over a long period of time. The stock market is good for long term investments to be sold at a later time, such as for mid-life, for retirement, and for your children when you pass on. When you start working, you can contribute to an Individual Retirement Account (IRA), which you set-up yourself at a brokerage firm. In addition, if your employer offers it, you can contribute to a 401K plan, a retirement plan, which is set-up for you by your employer with a brokerage firm, such as Fidelity. Mutual Funds, rather than individual company stocks, are typically purchased for retirement plans due to the perceived lower risk level, although this is not necessarily the case.

Before investing in the stock market, you must know what you are doing before undertaking such a risk, and it takes time to learn. I would recommend taking a class on investing in the stock market, assessing risk, and the fees involved in investing so that you are prepared for the future, whether you decide to invest yourself or hire a qualified "financial adviser." I would never invest in the stock market without knowing the basics of investing, without knowing how to assess risk of company stocks and mutual funds, without reading and understanding my contract with the brokerage firm, and without knowing the fees involved with each and every stock and mutual fund purchase and sale.

Investing in the stock market is exactly like gambling, and you cannot count on getting back any money you invest. You must know what you are doing.

money would only be worth $937,168, excluding inflation. While it sounds like a lot of money, you will need every bit of that, and more, to provide income for retirement age.

Please see **Table 7**, How Much You Can Save for Retirement. This table does not factor in inflation. This table is great for *estimating* how much you can save for the long term. In addition, you can use a table like this to *estimate* how much you can save for the short term, such as to save for a down payment on a home or a car. Using **Table 7**, run your own numbers in Excel to reflect your expected salary levels, savings levels, and realistic percentage gains for interest bearing accounts, real estate, mutual funds, stocks, and other investments, based on the career you choose. Some careers will allow you to make more money. The more money you make, the more money you can save and invest. The purpose of this exercise is to gain a broader understanding of how much money you can save, and what the savings might look like after 45 years, based on your chosen career. While this sounds overwhelming, you will see this is easy to do in Excel.

Through the help of a trusted, certified, and competent financial advisor, you will be able to find the right blend of investments, whether it is real estate, stocks, mutual funds, bonds, or other investment opportunities. However, always be wary of any opportunity and the costs involved. Sometimes the costs of managed mutual fund accounts or managed stock accounts are so high, you would have made more money letting the money earn interest in the bank. Sometimes illegal schemes can be peddled to you as well. Again, please be aware. If it sounds too good to be true, it is. Always investigate a company before handing over your money. This can easily be done by goggling the name of the company and/or person and entering "scam" or "scheme" or "trouble" or "complaint" or "lawsuit" or "bankruptcy" or any other fitting word you can think of. Also look for complaints on the www.ftc.gov website, the www.sec.gov website, the Better Business Bureau, your state Attorney General's office, any local government attorney offices, and any other appropriate websites. Spend some time doing your due diligence (research) before handing over your money. You will have worked too hard to lose your money.

Table 7
How Much You Can Save for Retirement

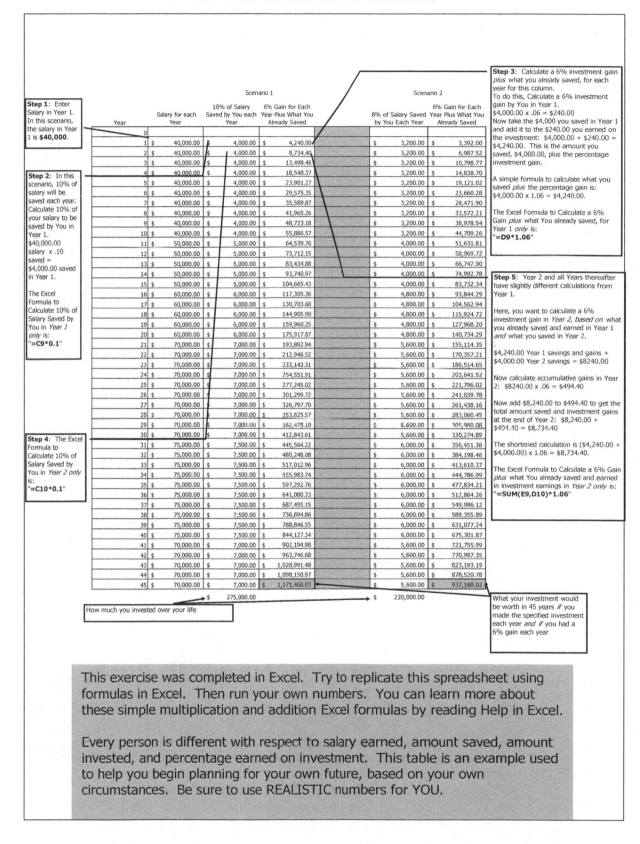

Step 1: Enter Salary in Year 1. In this scenario, the salary in Year 1 is **$40,000.**

Step 2: In this scenario, 10% of salary will be saved each year. Calculate 10% of your salary to be saved by You in Year 1. $40,000.00 salary x .10 saved = $4,000.00 saved in Year 1.

The Excel Formula to Calculate 10% of Salary Saved by You in Year 1 only is: **"=C9*0.1"**

Step 4: The Excel Formula to Calculate 10% of Salary Saved by You in Year 2 only is: **"=C10*0.1"**

Step 3: Calculate a 6% investment gain plus what you already saved, for each year for this column.
To do this, Calculate a 6% investment gain by You in Year 1.
$4,000.00 x .06 = $240.00
Now take the $4,000 you saved in Year 1 and add it to the $240.00 you earned on the investment: $4,000.00 + $240.00 = $4,240.00. This is the amount you saved, $4,000.00, plus the percentage investment gain.

A simple formula to calculate what you saved plus the percentage gain is: $4,000.00 x 1.06 = $4,240.00.

The Excel Formula to Calculate a 6% Gain plus what You already saved, for Year 1 only is: **"=D9*1.06"**

Step 5: Year 2 and all Years thereafter have slightly different calculations from Year 1.

Here, you want to calculate a 6% investment gain in Year 2, based on what you already saved and earned in Year 1 and what you saved in Year 2.

$4,240.00 Year 1 savings and gains + $4,000.00 Year 2 savings = $8240.00

Now calculate accumulative gains in Year 2: $8240.00 x .06 = $494.40

Now add $8,240.00 to $494.40 to get the total amount saved and investment gains at the end of Year 2: $8,240.00 + $494.40 = $8,734.40

The shortened calculation is ($4,240.00 + $4,000.00) x 1.06 = $8,734.40.

The Excel Formula to Calculate a 6% Gain plus what You already saved and earned in investment earnings in Year 2 only is: **"=SUM(E9,D10)*1.06"**

	Scenario 1				Scenario 2	
Year	Salary for each Year	10% of Salary Saved by You each Year	6% Gain for Each Year Plus What You Already Saved		8% of Salary Saved by You Each Year	6% Gain for Each Year Plus What You Already Saved
0						
1	$ 40,000.00	$ 4,000.00	$ 4,240.00		$ 3,200.00	$ 3,392.00
2	$ 40,000.00	$ 4,000.00	$ 8,734.40		$ 3,200.00	$ 6,987.52
3	$ 40,000.00	$ 4,000.00	$ 13,498.46		$ 3,200.00	$ 10,798.77
4	$ 40,000.00	$ 4,000.00	$ 18,548.37		$ 3,200.00	$ 14,838.70
5	$ 40,000.00	$ 4,000.00	$ 23,901.27		$ 3,200.00	$ 19,121.02
6	$ 40,000.00	$ 4,000.00	$ 29,575.35		$ 3,200.00	$ 23,660.28
7	$ 40,000.00	$ 4,000.00	$ 35,589.87		$ 3,200.00	$ 28,471.90
8	$ 40,000.00	$ 4,000.00	$ 41,965.26		$ 3,200.00	$ 33,572.21
9	$ 40,000.00	$ 4,000.00	$ 48,723.18		$ 3,200.00	$ 38,978.54
10	$ 40,000.00	$ 4,000.00	$ 55,886.57		$ 3,200.00	$ 44,709.26
11	$ 50,000.00	$ 5,000.00	$ 64,539.76		$ 4,000.00	$ 51,631.81
12	$ 50,000.00	$ 5,000.00	$ 73,712.15		$ 4,000.00	$ 58,969.72
13	$ 50,000.00	$ 5,000.00	$ 83,434.88		$ 4,000.00	$ 66,747.90
14	$ 50,000.00	$ 5,000.00	$ 93,740.97		$ 4,000.00	$ 74,992.78
15	$ 50,000.00	$ 5,000.00	$ 104,665.43		$ 4,000.00	$ 83,732.34
16	$ 60,000.00	$ 6,000.00	$ 117,305.36		$ 4,800.00	$ 93,844.29
17	$ 60,000.00	$ 6,000.00	$ 130,703.68		$ 4,800.00	$ 104,562.94
18	$ 60,000.00	$ 6,000.00	$ 144,905.90		$ 4,800.00	$ 115,924.72
19	$ 60,000.00	$ 6,000.00	$ 159,960.25		$ 4,800.00	$ 127,968.20
20	$ 60,000.00	$ 6,000.00	$ 175,917.87		$ 4,800.00	$ 140,734.29
21	$ 70,000.00	$ 7,000.00	$ 193,892.94		$ 5,600.00	$ 155,114.35
22	$ 70,000.00	$ 7,000.00	$ 212,946.52		$ 5,600.00	$ 170,357.21
23	$ 70,000.00	$ 7,000.00	$ 233,143.31		$ 5,600.00	$ 186,514.65
24	$ 70,000.00	$ 7,000.00	$ 254,551.91		$ 5,600.00	$ 203,641.52
25	$ 70,000.00	$ 7,000.00	$ 277,245.02		$ 5,600.00	$ 221,796.02
26	$ 70,000.00	$ 7,000.00	$ 301,299.72		$ 5,600.00	$ 241,039.78
27	$ 70,000.00	$ 7,000.00	$ 326,797.70		$ 5,600.00	$ 261,438.16
28	$ 70,000.00	$ 7,000.00	$ 353,825.57		$ 5,600.00	$ 283,060.45
29	$ 70,000.00	$ 7,000.00	$ 382,475.10		$ 5,600.00	$ 305,980.08
30	$ 70,000.00	$ 7,000.00	$ 412,843.61		$ 5,600.00	$ 330,274.89
31	$ 75,000.00	$ 7,500.00	$ 445,564.22		$ 6,000.00	$ 356,451.38
32	$ 75,000.00	$ 7,500.00	$ 480,248.08		$ 6,000.00	$ 384,198.46
33	$ 75,000.00	$ 7,500.00	$ 517,012.96		$ 6,000.00	$ 413,610.37
34	$ 75,000.00	$ 7,500.00	$ 555,983.74		$ 6,000.00	$ 444,786.99
35	$ 75,000.00	$ 7,500.00	$ 597,292.76		$ 6,000.00	$ 477,834.21
36	$ 75,000.00	$ 7,500.00	$ 641,080.33		$ 6,000.00	$ 512,864.26
37	$ 75,000.00	$ 7,500.00	$ 687,495.15		$ 6,000.00	$ 549,996.12
38	$ 75,000.00	$ 7,500.00	$ 736,694.86		$ 6,000.00	$ 589,355.89
39	$ 75,000.00	$ 7,500.00	$ 788,846.55		$ 6,000.00	$ 631,077.24
40	$ 75,000.00	$ 7,500.00	$ 844,127.34		$ 6,000.00	$ 675,301.87
41	$ 70,000.00	$ 7,000.00	$ 902,194.98		$ 5,600.00	$ 721,755.99
42	$ 70,000.00	$ 7,000.00	$ 963,746.68		$ 5,600.00	$ 770,997.35
43	$ 70,000.00	$ 7,000.00	$ 1,028,991.48		$ 5,600.00	$ 823,193.19
44	$ 70,000.00	$ 7,000.00	$ 1,098,150.97		$ 5,600.00	$ 878,520.78
45	$ 70,000.00	$ 7,000.00	$ 1,171,460.03		$ 5,600.00	$ 937,168.02
		$ 275,000.00			$ 220,000.00	

How much you invested over your life

What your investment would be worth in 45 years if you made the specified investment each year and if you had a 6% gain each year

This exercise was completed in Excel. Try to replicate this spreadsheet using formulas in Excel. Then run your own numbers. You can learn more about these simple multiplication and addition Excel formulas by reading Help in Excel.

Every person is different with respect to salary earned, amount saved, amount invested, and percentage earned on investment. This table is an example used to help you begin planning for your own future, based on your own circumstances. Be sure to use REALISTIC numbers for YOU.

Table 7 (Cont'd)
How Much You Can Save for Retirement
Excel Formulas

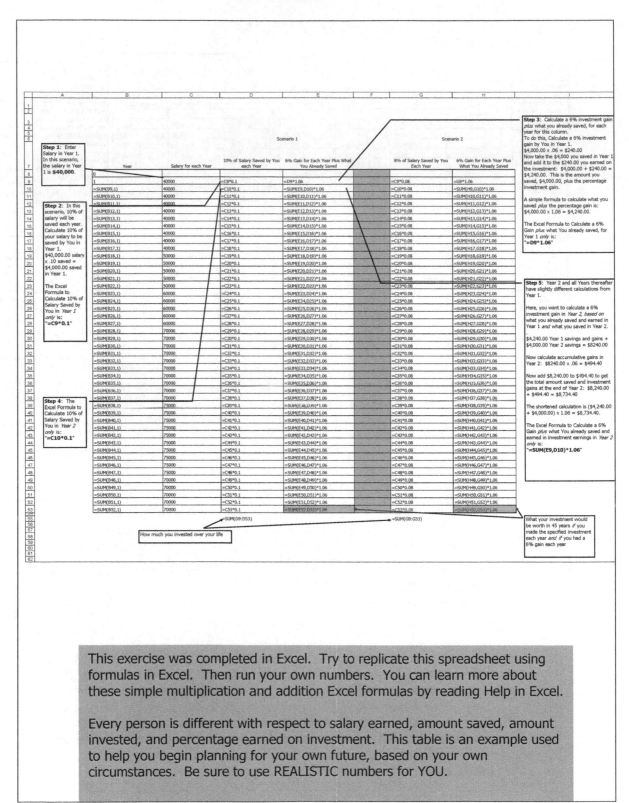

This exercise was completed in Excel. Try to replicate this spreadsheet using formulas in Excel. Then run your own numbers. You can learn more about these simple multiplication and addition Excel formulas by reading Help in Excel.

Every person is different with respect to salary earned, amount saved, amount invested, and percentage earned on investment. This table is an example used to help you begin planning for your own future, based on your own circumstances. Be sure to use REALISTIC numbers for YOU.

Learn to Manage a Budget

What is a budget? A budget is a specific amount of money that has been set aside to spend on a certain item, group of items, or service(s) for a period of time. Examples of budgets include a housing budget, expense budget, maintenance budget, grocery budget, entertainment budget, and vacation budget. These examples make up an overall household budget or Cost of Living Budget.

If we were to break down, say, a grocery budget, items that might be included would be specific food items, beverages, home cleansers, and shampoo. Your family may have a grocery budget of $150 per week. (The budget size will vary and depends on how many people you have in your family, if you live in a low cost or high cost area, how much money your family can afford to spend on food given income/salary level, other expenses, and savings plan.) If your family grocery budget is $150 per week, that means you have $150 to spend on food, beverages, home cleansers, shampoo, and other items.

To understand the thought and time it takes to manage a budget and the importance of managing a budget, I would recommend a parent or guardian assign you to manage the grocery budget for one week at a time for a couple of weeks throughout the year. To manage the grocery budget, this is what you need to do:

Step 1 - Know the budgeted amount and period of time (How much you are allowed to spend for all of the groceries within a week.)

Step 2 - Set-up three columns in an Excel spreadsheet: Item, Budgeted Amount, Actual Expenses. At the top of the Excel spreadsheet, enter the Total Budgeted Amount and period of time.

Step 3 - Make an itemized grocery shopping list by entering all of the items you need to purchase. Note a specific brand or an "or equal" brand to buy, if it matters. An "or equal" brand is known as a substitute. For example, there are different brands of milk, but milk tastes the same to me; so I always buy the cheapest milk.

Step 4 - Estimate how much each item on the shopping list will cost under the "Budgeted Amount" column. (You can do this by talking with your parents about their cost experience or by going to the store to create your own price sheet. Why not?)

Step 5 - Add the estimated Budgeted Amount column. Make sure the Total dollar amount is equal to or less than the Total Budgeted Amount for the one week period. Remove items from the list if you have to make the numbers work, but check with your parents first on what they can live without.

Step 6 - Go shopping with a parent or guardian as supervisor

Step 7 - After shopping, compare the Budgeted Amount with Actual Expenses by line item.

This is how a business manages a budget, comparing the budgeted amount with actual expenditures. The goal is to buy only items on the list and to spend equal to or less than the budgeted amount. Ideally you want the actual expenses to be as close to the budgeted amount as possible. You do not want to exceed the budget, $150 in this example, simply because you need to make sure you have enough money to pay the rent or mortgage. First and foremost, you must always have a roof over your head. Congratulations on managing your first budget!

Grocery Budget

Total Budgeted Amount _____ $150 _____ for _____ One Week Period _____

Item	Budgeted Amount (including tax)	Actual Expenses (including tax)
Milk	$4.00	$3.85
Eggs	$2.50	$2.25
Oatmeal	$4.00	$3.75
...	...	...
TOTAL:	Sum of this column	Sum of this column

When my husband and I were in college, we were very poor, as is the case with many college students. I remember one day we had just finished our last can of soup. We had absolutely no other food to eat, and we would not get paid for five days. Despite not having any food, we ended up going to the pool on this hot, summer day. Immediately when we got there, my husband dove into the pool, and at the very bottom of the deep end, he found a $10 bill. That $10 bought us enough groceries for an entire week! That would be the equivalent of approximately $20 today. I was never so happy to see spaghetti, soup, cold cuts and bread. Before going to the store, we made a list of all of the food items we could buy for $10 that would stretch for a five day period.

Today, what managing a budget means to me, is buying what is on the list for the least amount of money at the highest possible quality, and not spending more than the budgeted amount. If you are really good, you will not spend the entire amount in your budget, as this is money that can be used for something else or for savings.

Learn to Manage Money in a Checking Account and Savings Account

It is a good idea to establish a checking account in high school to understand what it takes to manage money and fees in an account, to read bank statements, and to reconcile your bank statement with your checkbook. Shop banks first to understand and compare the checking account fees involved so your money does not disappear before you have a chance to use it. Banks typically charge a fee to hold your money for you.

Once you have saved, say $500 or the minimum required by your bank, I would recommend opening a savings or money market account with no bank fees or charges, if available at the time. The bank will pay you interest on a savings and money market account. A money market account is similar to a savings account but may offer a higher interest rate than a savings account. A money market account usually has a limited number of checks you can write each month, whereas with a traditional savings account, you cannot write checks against the account. Be sure to shop for the highest interest rate and lowest fees for your savings account. Just as you would shop for the lowest price for a pair of the exact same shoes you want to buy in order to save money, here you want to find the highest interest rate with the lowest fees because you want to make the greatest amount of money possible.

One of your lifetime goals should be to have enough money in your checking account to cover any monthly bank fees, any checks you may want to write, and any debit card transactions. You should keep a copy of the checks you write and the original debit card receipts. I would recommend recording your transactions in your checkbook as you go and then balancing your checkbook with your bank statement each month. Many people do not do this. Do not fall into this trap. Banks and merchants (retailers) do make mistakes, and it is important to make sure the bank is not charging or over-charging you for fees. As I have experienced, sometimes a merchant (retailer) will accidently charge you twice. Also, you should make sure the bank is paying you the appropriate interest rate. I cannot tell you how much money I have saved over the years by doing this monthly audit. Any money the bank "takes" from me is less money saved by me.

Bouncing a check is wasted money on your part. As an example, if you write a check for $100 for shoes but only have $80 in your checking account, the bank will return the check to the merchant (the retailer) unpaid. If the bank charges you $30 for insufficient funds and the merchant charges you $30 for an unpaid check, you have lost $60. At this point, your account balance would be $20 without even paying for what you purchased. Now you are in trouble. Using this scenario, if you bounce a check 10 times over a year, it will cost you $600 in fees. That is $600 you could have saved to buy college books or pay your rent. You should keep in mind, intentionally bouncing a check is illegal. To learn how to reconcile a bank statement with your checkbook, please see **Table 8**.

When opening an account, be sure to protect yourself so that siblings and parents cannot take your money without your permission. The account representative at the bank will know how to do this.

Finally, be sure whichever bank you choose is insured by the Federal Deposit Insurance Corporation (FDIC). FDIC is a federal government entity that automatically insures money deposited in bank accounts, such as checking, savings, money market accounts, and certificates of deposit (CDs). (FDIC does NOT insure mutual funds, money market *funds*, stocks, bonds, life insurance policies, or annuities.) Cash deposits are insured up to $250,000 per person per financial institution. What this means is, if the bank goes out of business (becomes insolvent), you will still be able to withdraw your deposited money up to the insured amount per person, $250,000, provided you previously signed the signature card for each account you hold at the financial institution. You do not want to ever have more than the insured amount in one financial institution, because if the financial institution fails, you would lose the amount in excess of $250,000. To learn more about FDIC including which financial institutions are FDIC insured, which FDIC banks are solvent, and specific rules regarding insured accounts, please go to www.fdic.gov. Rules can change, and it is important to review the rules throughout your lifetime.

Credit Cards

Banks will try to entice you with credit cards. A credit card is a bank issued card that is used by you to purchase products and services. Rather than paying by cash or check, you pay by credit card with the promise to pay the bank in the future for the purchase you made. The bank pays the merchant (retailer, vendor).

Having a credit card can be a convenience. However, what is not convenient is charging more than the amount of money you have in your bank account. Traditionally, credit cards charge very high interest rates, such as 20% annually,

Table 8
Reconciling a Bank Statement with a Checkbook

My *bank statement* indicates the following transactions occurred in my checking account.

Beginning balance	$525.00
Ending balance	$300.00
Deposits	$150.00
Check# 1021	$113.98
ATM/Debit	$25.00
transactions	$54.87
	$25.00
	$41.72
	$83.44
	$30.99

My *checkbook* register shows the following entries:

Deposit on 8/01		**$150.00**
ATM on 8/02	**$25.00**	
Debit on 8/03	**$54.87**	
ATM on 8/4	**$25.00**	
Debit on 8/6	**$41.72**	
Debit on 8/15	**$83.44**	
Deposit on 8/15		**$100.00**
Debit on 8/20	**$30.99**	
ATM on 8/29	**$25.00**	
CURRENT BALANCE		**$375.00**

Table 8 (Cont'd)
Reconciling a Bank Statement with a Checkbook

To reconcile your bank statement with your checkbook, complete the following entries. You can do this.

1. Write down the Ending Balance from the bank statement

    Balance $_____

2. Write down the deposits **not** shown on the bank statement

Date	Amount	Date	Amount

3. Add the total deposits together in #2   Total $_____

4. Add #1 and #3 together   Total $_____

5. Write down all withdrawals, debit & ATM transactions, check transactions **not** found on this statement.

Check#/Date	Amount	Check#/Date	Amount

6. Add the total withdrawals together in #5   Total $_____

7. Subtract #6 from #4. This is your current balance and should match the balance in your checkbook.

    Total $_____

Table 8 (Cont'd)
Reconciling a Bank Statement with a Checkbook

ANSWERS

1. Write down the Ending Balance from the bank statement
                                                Balance $300.00

2. Write down the deposits **not** shown on the bank statement

Date	Amount	Date	Amount
8/15	$100.00		

3. Add the total deposits together in #2   Total $100.00

4. Add #1 and #3 together   Total $400.00

5. Write down all withdrawals, debit & ATM transactions,
   check transactions **not** found on this statement.

Check#/Date	Amount	Check#/Date	Amount
8/29 ATM	$25.00		

6. Add the total withdrawals together in #5   Total $25.00

7. Subtract #6 from #4. This is your current balance and should
   match the balance in your checkbook.
                                                Total $375.00

BERNTZEN

which may be compounded daily or monthly, depending on your contract. You may not realize this, but when you do not pay-off your credit card each month, you are actually borrowing money, and at a much higher rate than what you could get at your neighborhood bank.

Credit cards also require you to pay fees, expensive ones at that. Sometimes there is an annual fee just to have the card account, cash advance fee or a percentage of the transaction amount, foreign transaction fee or a percentage of the transaction amount, late payment fee, over-the-credit limit fee, return payment fee, return check fee, balance transfer from another credit card fee, and others.

If you are financially irresponsible, it will cost you a lot of money in interest and fees, making it extremely difficult for you to get back on track.

If I charged $2,500 on my credit card today and did not have the entire $2,500 to pay off the balance due at the end of the month, I would have to pay at the very least a minimum amount to the credit card company each month until I paid off the balance. The minimum amount would include interest and any principal (the amount I am borrowing) as required by the credit card company. Based on this scenario, compounded monthly, my monthly interest charge would be $41.66 ($2500 x (.2 interest/12 months)) for a $2,500 loan. In a 12 month period, if I did not pay principal but just paid interest, I would have paid the bank $500 ($41.66 monthly interest x 12 months) for a $2500 loan. That is outrageous! This is no way to live! (Many credit card companies use the Daily Balance Method, a daily compounding method, which means they calculate your daily balance and multiply it by your daily interest rate. See Reference 11. You can be sure daily compounding is more expensive than monthly compounding. You do the math.)

Shortly after I received my undergraduate degree, I met a young man in his 20's, making only $10,000 per year, who had maxed-out all of his credit cards to $40,000. I do not know how he was technically able to have a $40,000 credit line. At a 20% interest rate per year, it would have cost him $666.67 per month or $8,000 per year in *interest alone*, without paying any principal down! He did not know what to do, was depressed, and was considering filing for bankruptcy.

Today, you cannot escape your debt as easily. According to the Federal Trade Commission's website, if you file for bankruptcy, it remains on your credit record for a period of ten years, and it harms your ability to get a loan or a low interest loan during that period of time. If you file for bankruptcy, you will still have to pay your student loans, credit card loans, taxes, alimony, and child support. If you cross this path, there will be ruthless lenders out there to take advantage of you and charge very high interest rates and fees for any loans you seek, such as car loans. Borrowing money at very high interest rates will make it almost impossible to get out of the hole. It is not worth it to run up your credit card beyond what you can afford. It can ruin your life financially, emotionally, spiritually, can ruin relationships, and work opportunities.

Remember to review your credit card statement each month for inaccuracies. Be sure to save your credit card receipts as you go so you can properly review your monthly credit card statement. Many people think a bogus $10 charge on their credit card will not hurt them, and they pay it for whatever reason. However, over a lifetime, this can add up to several thousand dollars. When you spot these bogus charges, you should call your credit card company to contest it immediately. Also, many credit card companies are submitting checks electronically, and on occasion the amounts are entered incorrectly. This means, more money could be deducted from your checking account than you planned. (This is yet another reason to reconcile your checkbook with your bank statement.) I experienced writing a check to a credit card company at say, $1000, which was entered and filed electronically at $100,000. This obviously got my and my bank's attention immediately. Several years later, I am still waiting for an apology from the credit card company. If you are wondering if this affected my credit record, it did not. I addressed it immediately with both the bank and the credit card company, and I followed-up repeatedly on both ends throughout this three week fiasco to ensure I was provided with consistent information, that it would not affect my credit record.

As a last note, it is better to pay for an online purchase with a credit card than it is to pay with a debit card. If someone steals your credit card, your maximum liability (loss) is $50. However, you need to report it immediately to the credit card company. If someone steals your debit card, your maximum liability (loss) is *unlimited*, if you fail to report it to your bank within 60 days. If you report your debit card as stolen within two business days, your maximum liability is $50. If you report your debit card as stolen, between three days and 60 days, you are responsible for $500. As a general rule, you should report any lost or stolen credit cards or debit cards within 24 hours. Banks will try to sell you credit card insurance if your credit card is lost or stolen, but please know, as a consumer, you already have limited liability under the law. Laws change frequently. For more information and for the most updated information on credit card and debit card liability, go to www.ftc.gov.

Purchasing a Home

Learning about purchasing a home now may seem way far out, but I want to give you a few basic tips to help prepare you for purchasing a home. Upon reading this section and the following section, *What it Costs to Live*, you will see why it is important for you to know this now.

It is important to remember that housing prices vary from location to location. Typically, larger cities are more expensive than smaller cities and rural areas. As previously mentioned, if you live in Chicago, the median price of a home is about $199,200, and if you live in Corpus Christi, Texas, the median price of a home today is approximately $134,300. Usually salaries are higher in high cost areas, and are a bit lower in lower cost areas, but not always.

According to the Federal Housing Administration (FHA) website, "monthly mortgage payments should be no more than 31% of gross income." (Gross income is your pre-tax salary. To say it another way, gross income is your salary before paying taxes. For example, an employer hires you at $50,000 per year to be an electrical engineer. Your gross income then is $50,000, which is your salary before taxes are paid. Again, $50,000 is your pre-tax salary.) In addition to mortgage payments, I would recommend including the following "housing" costs in this category: property taxes, homeowner's insurance, any flood insurance, homeowner's association or condo fees, any mortgage insurance, and any other fees and insurance associated with owning a home.

The FHA also states "housing" *and* "non-housing" or long term obligations should not be more than 43% of your total gross income. Long term obligations include any credit card loans, car loans, student loans, alimony, child support, and other outstanding loans and long term obligations.

You should know, under traditional terms, to purchase a home will require a 10% down payment of the loan value, and the life of the loan will be 30 years. (While some lenders are now offering 40 year loans, I would not recommend taking out a loan greater than 30 years, because it costs you a lot more money in interest over the life of the loan. It is a good deal for the lender but not for you.) Let's say, if the purchase price of your first home is $100,000, you will need to have saved $10,000 in order to make a down payment of 10% ($100,000 purchase price x .10 down payment multiplier = $10,000 down payment). With traditional mortgages, you cannot borrow the down payment for a home.

If you are able to make a down payment of 20%, and congratulations to you if you can, then you will not have to pay monthly mortgage insurance.

Currently, according to the FHA website, mortgage insurance can cost you .5% per month times the loan amount. In this case, $100,000 purchase price x (.005 mortgage insurance / 12 months) = $41.66 per month. Your mortgage insurance would be approximately $500 per year if you paid less than 20% down. In 10 years, that is $5,000 that you could have saved or used for something else. If you pay down less than 20%, then you should know that once you have paid in 20% of your loan, you should no longer have to pay mortgage insurance. Be sure to find this clause in your mortgage contract before you sign the contract. When you reach the 20% mark, if your lender has not sent you a new payment booklet, you will need to contact your lender in writing. Do *not* withhold money without *written* documentation from the lender as this can be perceived as a non-payment, and it will come back to haunt you.

You need to be conscious of how much it costs to purchase a home and all expenses involved in living.

What it Costs to Live

I would like to use FHA's housing formula to help us develop a Cost of Living Budget, because the formula works fairly well with a little tweaking. Of course, how well it works depends on your circumstances such as if you live in a high cost or low cost area. To develop a Cost of Living Budget, you can divide your budget into three parts: "housing" (no more than 31% of gross income, also known as pre-tax income), "non-housing" long-term obligations (no more than 12% of gross income), and "other" (57% of gross income = 100% - 31% - 12%). "Housing" and "non-housing" long term obligations should *not* total more than 43% of your total gross income. I should say, dedicating exactly 31% of your gross income to "housing" and 12% of your gross income to "non-housing" long term obligations can be high, as you will see from the below example. However, it all depends on your circumstances and how much it costs to live in your area. These percentages are only offered as a guideline and ultimately what you budget and spend is up to you; however, please do not go over the "housing" and "non-housing" recommended percentages, because having too much debt can impact your ability to live a comfortable life and can impact your ability to get a loan for something you really want in the future. With that said, I would recommend you spend a lot less on "housing" and "non-housing" long-term obligations, as you will have more wiggle room to pay unexpected expenses, such as a doctor's or dentist's bill, and to save money for short-term and long-term needs. While reading the below Cost of Living

64

Budget definitions and example, I encourage you to review the Cost of Living Budget format in **Table 9**. See pages 159 and 160 to set your Personal Lifetime Standard.

"Housing" includes your apartment rent or mortgage payment if you purchased the home, homeowner's association or condo fees, renter's insurance or homeowner's insurance, any flood insurance, mortgage insurance if you purchased the property at less than 20% down, property taxes if you own the property, and any other obligations associated with owning a home or renting.

"Non-housing" and long term obligations would include any credit card loans, car loans, student loans, alimony, child support, and other outstanding loans and long term obligations.

The "other" category includes Taxes, Living Expenses, and long-term and short-term Savings. Taxes include local income taxes, state income taxes, federal income taxes, social security taxes, Medicare, and Medicaid. All of these taxes are deducted from your paycheck and hopefully in the correct amounts which you need to verify through your employer at the beginning of each year. Living Expenses include car insurance, health insurance, medical expenses not covered by health insurance, food/groceries, fuel for your car, entertainment, cable, high speed internet access, phone, cell phone, water, trash service, gas, electricity, clothes, shoes, dry cleaning, and other obligations. Savings includes what you want to save in the short-term and long-term for furniture, down payment for a car and home, electronics, home maintenance such as a new roof, and retirement. Throughout your life, you should save and have cash on hand for one year of "housing," "non-housing," and "other" (taxes and required living expenses) obligations in order to protect yourself should you lose your job.

If you make $40,000 per year, using the formula, you can have a maximum annual "housing" budget of $12,400 per year ($40,000 x .31 or 31% = $12,400.) or $1,033.33 per month ($12,400 / 12 months = $1,033.33).

That means your "non-housing" long term obligations can be no more than 12% of your gross income (43% - 31% = 12%) or $4,800 per year ($40,000 x .12 or 12% = $4,800) or $400 per month ($4,800 / 12 months = $400).

Your "other" expenses can be no more than 57% of your gross income (100% - 12% - 31% = 57%) or $22,800 per year ($40,000 x .57 or 57% = $22,800) or $1,900 per month ($22,800 / 12 = $1,900). Before you get too excited, much of that money will go to taxes. Under current tax laws, if you are not married, do not have any children, do not have any deductions, no one can claim you as a dependent, and you make $40,000 per year, your federal income taxes will be

Table 9

Cost of Living Budget

Please read the instructions on pages 159 and 160 before completing this form.

This budget is based on the Federal Housing Administration's (FHA's) housing formula and should be used as a guideline only.

"Housing" and "Non-housing" long term obligations should *not* total more than 43% of your total gross income, based on FHA's formula.

I would recommend you spend much less than 43% of your total gross income on "Housing" and "Non-housing" to keep your debt low, maintain a good credit score, and keep your options open.

My gross income is _____ per year.

My gross income is _____ per month.

(Gross income is also known as pre-tax income.)

"Housing" Obligations

"Housing" obligations should be **no more than 31% of gross income**, based on FHA's formula.

31% of my gross income is equal to _____.

My "Housing" obligations can be no more than $_____ per month or $_____ per year.

Personal Lifetime Standard. According to my Personal Lifetime Standard, my "Housing" obligations can be no more than _____% of my gross income. That means, I can spend no more than $_____ per month or $_____ per year on "Housing" obligations.

	Monthly	Annually
Apartment Rent or Mortgage loan payment if you purchased a home		
Homeowner's Association fees or Condo fees (Generally, this is for maintenance and upkeep of the grounds and building)		
Renter's Insurance if you rent or Homeowner's Insurance if you purchased a home		
Flood Insurance or other required insurance		
Mortgage Insurance if you purchased a home and you put less than 20% down on the purchase price of the home		
Property taxes, if you purchased the property (If you rent a property, the owner pays property taxes.)		
Any land lease fees (Sometimes a home purchased sits on property that belongs to someone else, and consequently, the homeowner must pay land lease fees. This is not very common but you should make sure any home you purchase does not require you to lease the land.)		
TOTAL		

"Non-housing" Obligations

"Non-housing" obligations should be **no more than 12% of gross income**, based on FHA's formula.

12% of my gross income is equal to _____.

My "Non-housing" obligations can be no more than $_____ per month or $_____ per year

Personal Lifetime Standard. According to my Personal Lifetime Standard, my "Housing" obligations can be no more than _____% of my gross income. That means, I can spend no more than $_____ per month or $_____ per year on "Housing" obligations.

	Monthly	Annually
Student Loan Payment		
Credit Card Loan Payment (If you do not pay off your credit card each month, this is considered a loan. Borrowing from your credit card can make it difficult to pay-off, because interest rates are often around 20% per year.)		
Car Loan Payment		
Alimony		
Child Support		
Other loans and long term obligations		
TOTAL		

"Other" Obligations

The "Other" obligations include obligations to yourself, such as for savings, and to others. **If you spend exactly 31% of gross income on "Housing" and exactly 12% of gross income on "Non-housing" then you would spend 57% of your gross income on "Other" obligations.** The total percentages of these three categories must add up to 100%, otherwise you will get yourself into trouble. (100% - 31% - 12% = 57%).

____% of my gross income is equal to _____.

My "other" obligations can be no more than _____ per month or _____ per year.

TAXES (Taxes are deducted from your paycheck automatically. You will need to verify the taxes are withheld in the correct amounts each month. You will need to consider taxes when budgeting.)	Monthly	Annually
Federal Income Taxes (Internal Revenue Service)		
State Income Taxes (This is the state in which you live and work. State income taxes can be zero or high, such as 5.5%.)		
Local Income Taxes (This is the township or city in which you live and work. Not all localities have income taxes.)		
Social Security and Medicare Taxes (This is currently a flat rate of 7.65% of income received from an employer.)		
Medicaid (This is specific to the state in which you live and work. Not all states have Medicaid and not all states tax for Medicaid through income.)		

Table 9 (Cont'd)

Cost of Living Budget

"Other" Obligations (Cont'd)

SAVINGS - Short Term and Long Term	Monthly	Annually
Short Term		
One (1) Year of "housing," "non-housing," and "other" (taxes you owe, and required living expenses) obligations from your expected budget should be saved throughout your lifetime. You should have this as cash on hand. -- I need to save a total of $_____. I plan to save the total amount within _____ months.		
Down payment for a car. -- I need to save a total of $_____. I plan to save the total amount within _____ months.		
Down payment for a home (10% or 20% of the purchase price). -- I need to save a total of $_____. I plan to save the total amount within _____ months.		
Nice furniture to last a lifetime. -- I need to save a total of $_____. I plan to save the total amount within _____ months.		
Home maintenance, such as painting and a new roof. -- I need to save a total of $_____. I plan to save the total amount within _____ months.		
Home electronics. -- I need to save a total of $_____. I plan to save the total amount within _____ months.		
Vacation. -- I need to save a total of $_____. I plan to save the total amount within _____ months.		
Other needs. -- I need to save a total of $_____. I plan to save the total amount within _____ months.		
Other needs. -- I need to save a total of $_____. I plan to save the total amount within _____ months.		
Long Term - Retirement		
IRA (Individual Retirement Account). You set-up an IRA account through a brokerage firm and can contribute up to a certain amount per year as required by law.		
401k. You and your employer contribute to a 401k retirement account that is set-up for you with a brokerage firm. Your employer may match a certain percentage of what you contribute. (Include only your contributions here. Do not include your employer's contributions here.)		
Stock or Mutual Fund Account through a brokerage firm		
Cash held in an interest bearing account		

EXPENSES	Monthly	Annually
Car Insurance		
Health Insurance		
Medical expenses including prescriptions not covered by health insurance		
Food / Groceries		
Fuel for Car		
Entertainment and Dining Out		
Cable		
High Speed Internet Access		
Land line phone		
Cell phone		
Water service		
Trash service		
Gas service		
Electricity		
Clothes		
Shoes		
Laundry and Dry cleaning		
Other needs and obligations		
Other needs and obligations		
Other needs and obligations		
Other needs and obligations		
TOTAL (Taxes, Savings, Expenses)		

	Monthly	Annually
TOTAL OBLIGATIONS ("Housing", "Non-housing", and "Other" Obligations)		
GROSS INCOME (from the top of the worksheet)		

For Budgeting purposes, Total Obligations should equal Gross Income. (You must always consider the cost of taking loans including fees, penalties such as paying off a loan early, and interest rates. High interest rates, starting at 10% can keep you in the hole longer and interest rates at 15% or higher can bankrupt you, depending on how much you make and how much you borrowed.) Any interest you pay to a credit card company is less money you could have saved for short term or long term purchases.

$4,345. I know this by completing the IRS 1040EZ form. That makes the federal effective tax rate 10.8625% on $40,000 ($4,345 / $40,000 = .108625 x 100% = 10.8625%). The federal effective tax rate is the total amount paid in federal income taxes divided by your total gross income, that is, income before taxes. Calculating the effective tax rate is just a way of understanding how much you pay in taxes with respect to your gross income. The social security and Medicare tax rate is a flat tax rate for all employees and the employee's share is currently 7.65% of salary. The employer also pays 7.65% of your salary to social security and Medicare, also known as FICA. In summary, the government receives 7.65% + 7.65% = 15.30% of your salary for social security and Medicare. (Please note: If you are working now, you will notice in 2011, your FICA is reduced by 2% but will go back up to 7.65% in 2012. Reducing the FICA flat tax rate by 2% for everyone should increase *disposable income* in the aggregate economy, which means, we should spend and save more money. The government is hoping we will spend more money, because theoretically, this may help bring our economy out of its long recession.) Your 7.65% share translates to $3,060 per year on a $40,000 income. Some states have Medicaid tax deducted from your paycheck. See **Table 10**, Social Security, Medicare, and Medicaid. In this scenario, I estimate about a 2.5% state and local income tax rate or $1000 ($40,000 x .025 = $1000). This percentage will vary by the state, and some states do not have state income taxes; however, you may be taxed in other ways such as higher property taxes or motor vehicle registration fees. In this scenario, your total salary tax obligation on a $40,000 annual income would be 21.0125%. (10.8625% effective federal income tax rate + 7.65% social security and Medicare tax rate + 2.5% effective state income tax rate = 21.0125%.) Yes, that is correct.

Given your salary tax obligation of 21.0125% or $8,405 per year or $700.42 per month, your "other" expenses can now be *no more than* $1,199.58 per month ($1,900 - $700.42 = $1,199.58).

To review, in this scenario, you would spend 31% of your gross income on "housing," 12% on "non-housing" long term obligations, and 57% on "other" expenses. After paying taxes on salary, you are left with 35.9874% ($1,199.58 x 12 months = $14,394.96 / $40,000 = .359874 x 100 = 35.9874%) of your total gross income or $14,394.96 per year. A total of $1,199.58 per month ($14,394.96 / 12 months = $1,199.58) is available for "other" obligations.

If you decide you want to save 10% of your gross income or $4,000 per year ($40,000 x .10 = $4,000), that leaves $10,394 ($14,394 - $4,000 = $10,394) for

Table 10

Social Security, Medicare, and Medicaid

Social Security is a federal program that delivers income to those who are retired and to the disabled. Social Security is deducted from our paycheck today, and it immediately pays benefits to retirees and the disabled. Benefits are minimal, depending on your situation, and are expected to be reduced in 2041 without any law or policy changes. Social Security is intended only as a supplement to your own retirement savings. However, with that said, I would not factor in Social Security as a part of your income when you retire. Any Social Security you receive when you retire will be a bonus. You can read about Social Security at the Social Security Administration's website www.ssa.gov or www.socialsecurity.gov.

Medicare is a federal health insurance program for the elderly and for some disabled.

FICA (Federal Insurance Contributions Act) is the combination of social security taxes and Medicare taxes we pay. These are also known as payroll taxes to employers. Social Security and Medicare taxes usually show up as FICA taxes on your paycheck.

Medicaid is a federal and state health insurance program for the poor. Not all states have Medicaid.

"other" expenses for one year or $866 per month. Again, $866 per month can be used on cable, internet, phone, cell phone, gas, electricity, health insurance, medical expenses not covered under health insurance, water, food, fuel for your car, entertainment, clothes, vacations and other obligations.

I have to say, if I made $40,000 using this scenario, I would elect to spend a lot less on "housing" and/or "non-housing" obligations, because I know from experience that $866 per month for "other" expenses will be a very tight squeeze to pay all obligations, unless you do without cable, high speed internet, land line phone, entertainment, new clothes, and so forth. Cable, high speed internet, and land line phone can cost approximately $150 per month depending on where you live. Water, electricity, gas can cost several hundred dollars per month for a smaller home or apartment. Car insurance can cost about $100 per month, depending on the car, your age, and your driving record. Health insurance alone can cost around $150 or $1150 per month depending on your health status and your employer's plan. Fuel for your car can cost very little if you live near where you work or several hundred dollars per month if you live far from your job.

As you can see, budgeting is a very complex process, but it can be done and should be done to ensure you have enough money to pay your obligations and have enough money for today and your future. Some things I would recommend to help keep your budget on track:

- Before obtaining a student loan, be sure there is alignment between how much you are borrowing, your monthly payments due after college, and your expected monthly salary after graduation. Be sure to use the Cost of Living Budget to do this. You should calculate what your expected monthly loan payments would be, before taking out a student loan. See **Table 11**, Calculating Loan Payments. Also, you can obtain the expected salary information from your College, Career, and Money Plan. For example, if you take out $100,000 in student loans but your expected annual salary when you graduate is $25,000, you would not be able to make your student loan payments and rent a decent apartment. You would be broke. Remember, one of the reasons for going to college is to support yourself.

- Throughout your life, you should save and have cash on hand to cover one year of "housing," "non-housing," and "other" (taxes and required living expenses) obligations from the Cost of Living Budget in order to protect yourself should you lose your job. This is another good reason to live beneath your means.

- Never, ever obligate yourself to any large purchase without running the numbers in your budget to ensure you truly can afford it. You are the best judge of what you can afford. Remember, this is your life!

- Estimate your federal, state, and local income tax obligations at the beginning of each year for budgeting purposes.

- *Before* buying a home, estimate the cost of property taxes as assessed by the county where the home is located, homeowner's association or condo fees, homeowner's insurance, any flood insurance required or needed, any mortgage insurance, and any other obligations. Depending on location, size, cost of the home, these expenses can run several thousand dollars per year. Also look at past history of water, electric and gas bills to estimate how much you might owe if you owned the home. Every home is different and uses varying degrees of utilities. Learn if there are any liens on the home you are trying to buy. (A lien is an obligation to pay someone money, such as a homeowner's association if the owner failed to pay monthly fees.) Review the homeowner's association rules to ensure the home is currently within compliance. Read and understand the seller's contract, available from the real estate agent listing the home. Understand the condition of the home. Hire a qualified home inspector. Estimate the amount needed for annual home maintenance, a new roof, painting, new driveway, landscaping, etc. Be sure to run the numbers in your budget to see if you can afford the home *before* you make an offer. See **Table 11**, Calculating Loan Payments.

- *Before* buying a car, ask your insurance agent how much the insurance premium would cost. Car insurance premiums vary by the type of car and of course, the driver. Also, and very importantly, make sure you have auto insurance coverage from the moment you sign the loan documents on your car. I know someone who bought a car, did not have insurance coverage, and totaled the car on his way home from the car dealer. He was set back financially for a period of time. The good news is, he was not hurt.

- I would never do without health insurance because should you become ill or be in an unexpected accident, your medical expenses can bankrupt you. One trip to the Emergency Room today can cost around $1200. A lengthy hospital stay can cost in the tens of thousands of dollars. Be sure you understand the fine print on what is covered and what is not, before you sign-up with a health insurance plan. You will be obligated to pay your medical bills, and any bills paid late or not paid will go on your credit record. See the section below, Establishing a Credit Score to Get a Home Loan or Car Loan.

- In general, estimate your expected expenses and run the numbers in your Cost of Living Budget to see if you can afford it, before taking on the obligation of those expenses.

You can use the Cost of Living Budget to develop your own estimated Cost of Living Budget for the future such as for college planning and life planning after college. A completed example of the Cost of Living Budget is provided at the end of this book.

Establishing a Credit Score to Get a Home Loan or Car Loan

How do you establish a credit history? Every time you pay your bills such as a student loan, car loan, mortgage, credit card bill, utility bill, hospital bill, or any bill for that matter, you are establishing your credit history. You are establishing a *good* credit history when you pay your bills on time, you decide to keep your bank account balanced (not overdrawing the account), have a credit card in your own name and keep the account current, limit the number of credit cards and maximum credit limits you have, and limit the number of times your credit record is checked by financial institutions and brokerage firms. To determine if you are a low risk or high risk customer, financial institutions will check your credit history when you open a bank account, apply for a credit card, or apply for any type of loan. Brokerage firms will check your credit history when you open an account. Your credit history establishes your credit score.

The three credit reporting agencies, Equifax, Experian, and Trans Union, use your credit history along with your income to calculate your credit score. Ultimately, your credit score determines whether you get a low interest loan or a high interest loan for a car or home. Credit reporting agencies do this for everyone, and you cannot opt out. Just as a business is assigned a credit rating, each person is assigned a credit rating or credit score.

If you do not pay your bills on time, this will impact your credit score. If you have high loan amounts (including what you owe on credit cards) compared with how much money you make, this can impact your credit score. If you have many credit cards, used or not, this can impact your credit score. Your credit score will determine the interest rate offered to you and consequently whether you can afford to purchase the home of your choice or a home at all. Again, all bills must be paid by the due date listed on each bill. In other words, the biller must receive payment *before* the due date. If someone tells you it is okay to pay a utility bill one day before the electricity is to be shut off, know this is not how it should be for someone who wants to live in peace. My advice is to snail mail your payment at least seven days before the due date on the bill, or pay three to four days in advance by phone or electronically with a secure line, as long as there is not a "convenience fee." Again, you must have money in your checking account to cover all bills to be paid. The money in your checking account comes from your salary and savings.

Guard Your Personal Information

My goal is to help you start thinking about protecting your finances, and it begins with protecting your personal information. Be careful *not* to share your social security number and other identifying information such as your driver's license number, bank account number, mother's maiden name, father's middle name, and birth date with anyone outside of a legitimate bank with which you have applied for a loan. Social security numbers historically are used for administration of social security benefits for retirement and disability, college applications, employer background checks, life insurance, taxes, and health insurance plans through employers as well as securing loans and credit cards. Some employers will ask you for your social security number on a job application. My advice is not to give your social security number or driver's license number to a prospective employer unless you applied for a job with the company, you learned it is a reputable company as evidenced by your internet research, *and* you have a written job offer. A legitimate and savvy employer will understand it is important not to provide a social security number prior to a job offer.

The Federal Trade Commission recommends checking your credit report at least once each year, and this should apply to teens as well. It is a good idea to begin checking your credit report when you are a Sophomore in high school. That way, you can make sure no one has taken out a loan in your name, known as identity theft, before you begin applying for any student loans. You can check your credit report for free through the Federal Trade Commission's website, www.ftc.gov/freereports, as it is the official government website for consumer protection, and the FTC's website will refer you to its approved source for providing a free credit report, www.AnnualCreditReport.com. I would avoid responding to any advertisements on television, radio, internet, e-mail, mail, billboard, fax, phone or other avenue that use your social security number as a tool to get information, such as a credit report. The reason is, you do not know if the advertiser is a legitimate and honorable business.

As a final note, if you have not already done so, I recommend installing a good firewall with virus and spyware protection on your computer at home, the one with which you connect to the internet. You should also access the internet from a non-administrator account. I would not store any documents with confidential and personal identifying information such as a social security number, driver's license number, or bank account number on a computer that connects to the internet.

Table 11

Calculating Loan Payments

      This formula can be used to calculate loan payments for any type of loan when the interest rate is *fixed* or *adjustable*, such as for student loans, home mortgage loans, and car loans. A fixed interest rate means the interest rate is the same throughout the life of the loan. An adjustable interest rate means the interest rate can change during the life of the loan (loan term) and is based on a key economic indicator in the marketplace, such as the prime rate, over which you have no control. I do not recommend adjustable interest rate loans, because your future payments are always unknown. When you use the below formulas for an adjustable interest rate, just know the calculation is only good for the interest rate you plug into it. When the rate changes, re-do the calculation with the new interest rate.

      Everyone should know how to calculate loan payments themselves, as it is important for the planning process. I like to use "what if" scenarios, such as, if I can buy this car for $20,000 (or $21,000 or $22,000, etc.) and I can get an interest rate of 3% (or 2.9% or 2.8%, etc.), then I can afford the car. However, I understand the greater the number of payments made over the life of the loan (loan term), the more money I have to pay in interest to the financial institution. This is a very powerful formula, and it is easy to learn. You can use a calculator or use Excel to make your calculations. At the end of this table, I will show you the formulas for calculating it in Excel.

$$\text{Loan Amount} \times \frac{(1 + i)^n \times i}{(1 + i)^n - 1} = \text{Payment Amount Due Per Month}$$

Loan Amount = Principal = Amount You are Borrowing

$$i = \frac{\text{interest rate expressed as a decimal (i.e. 5\% interest is expressed as .05)}}{\text{number of payments to be made each year}}$$

n = Number of Payments to be made over the life of the loan

Example 1

      I plan to borrow a total of $100,000 to get a bachelor's and master's degree from an expensive school, but I am not sure I can afford the loan payments based on the $25,000 I expect to receive in salary after graduating from college. I learned I can choose to pay back the loan within 10 years or 20 years. I have shopped around and I know the lowest *fixed* interest rate I can get right now is 6%. Using the formula from above:

10 year Loan

$$\$100,000 \times \frac{(1 + .06/12)^{120} \times .06/12}{(1 + .06/12)^{120} - 1} = \$1,110.21 \text{ Monthly Payment}$$

This means *each month* over a 10 year period, I will have to pay $1,110.21 toward my student loan.

Total Amount Paid in Student Loans = Monthly Payment x n

$133,224.60 = $1,110.21 x 120

Total Amount Paid in Interest = Total Amount Paid in Student Loans − Principal

$33,224.60 = $133,224.60 - $100,000

20 year Loan

$$\$100{,}000 \ \times \ \frac{(1 + .06/12)^{240} \times .06/12}{(1 + .06/12)^{240} - 1} = \$716.43 \text{ Monthly Payment}$$

This means *each month* over a 20 year period, I will have to pay $716.43 toward my student loan.

Total Amount Paid in Student Loans = Monthly Payment x n

$171,943.45 = $716.43 x 240

Total Amount Paid in Interest = Total Amount Paid in Student Loans − Principal

$71,943.45 = $171,943.45- $100,000

Analysis:

Notice the total amount of interest paid after 20 years is more than double what it was after 10 years. This tells me the longer the loan term, the more money I have to pay in interest. This is always the case with a *fixed* interest rate loan. This is money I could have saved for a down payment on a home or saved for retirement.

Using the Cost of Living Budget, if I make $25,000 in salary after college, my monthly gross salary is $25,000 / 12 = $2083.33. I know from the Cost of Living Budget that "housing" and "non-housing" obligations should not total more than 43% of my gross income. 43% of my gross annual income is .43 x $25,000 = $10,750 or $10,750 / 12 = $895.83 per month. From these calculations, I know that with a 10 year loan my monthly payments would be $1,110.21, which is above $895.83. I cannot afford this loan at a 10 year repayment plan, and I will not have any money for housing/apartment rent or a car. With a 20 year loan my monthly payments would be $716.43. While $716.43 is less than $895.83 per month, I would still not be able to afford adequate housing at $179.40 per month ($895.83 - $716.43= $179.40) and I would not be able to afford a car.

Taking out a $100,000 loan when I expect to make $25,000 in salary could bankrupt me. I will not be able to afford to live on my own after college if I take out a $100,000 loan. At this point, I should look at other high quality schools that are a lot less expensive.

Example 2

I would like to buy a $35,000 car when I graduate from college. I have $1,000 I can use as a down payment, which means I would borrow $34,000. I can get a 5 year car loan at a 5% interest rate. Using the same formula:

$34,000 Loan

$$\$34,000 \ \times \ \frac{(1 + .05/12)^{60} \times .05/12}{(1 + .05/12)^{60} - 1} = \$641.62 \text{ Monthly Payment}$$

My monthly payment for a 5 year, $34,000 loan is $641.62.

Total Amount Paid for the Loan = Monthly Payment x   n
$38,497.32 = $641.62 x 60

Total Amount Paid in Interest = Total Amount Paid for the Loan – Principal
$4,497.32 = $38,497.32 - $34,000

Now I will compare the cost of buying a $25,000 car with a $1,000 down payment, which means I would borrow $24,000. My loan term is 5 years and the interest rate is 5%.

$24,000 Loan

$$\$24,000 \ \times \ \frac{(1 + .05/12)^{60} \times .05/12}{(1 + .05/12)^{60} - 1} = \$452.91 \text{ Monthly Payment}$$

My monthly payment for a 5 year, $24,000 loan is $452.91.

Total Amount Paid for the Loan = Monthly Payment x   n
$27,174.58 = $452.91 x 60

Total Amount Paid in Interest = Total Amount Paid for the Loan – Principal
$3,174.58= $27,174.58 - $24,000

Analysis:

In this example, my annual salary is $50,000. (This is my pre-tax income or gross income.) My apartment rent is $700 per month and my renter's insurance is $40 per month. I do not have any other "housing" or "non-housing" obligations. From the Cost of Living Budget, I know I *cannot* spend more than 43% of my gross income on "housing" and "non-housing" obligations. 43% of $50,000 is $21,500 per year (.43 x $50,000 = $21,500) or $1,791.66 per month ($21,500 / 12 months = $1,791.66). I know that $740 is way under the $1,791.66 limit that I can spend. In fact, $740 is 17.76% of my gross income ($740 / ($50,000 / 12 months) = .1776). If I had a monthly car payment of $641.62, my rent was $700 per month, and my renter's insurance was $40 per month, my total "housing" and "non-housing" obligations would be $1,381.62 ($641.62 + $700 + $40 = $1,381.62). $1,381.62 is 33.15% of my gross income ($1,481.62 / ($50,000 / 12 months) = .3315). I am roughly 10% under my limit of 43%.

Because I would like to save money to buy a home and nice furniture in the future, I decided I would buy a $25,000 car instead of a $35,000 car. The difference in my monthly payments is $188.71. By buying a $25,000 car instead of a $35,000 car, in a five year period, I can save $11,322.60 ($188.71 x 60 months = $11,322.60).

Example 3

      I plan to take out a mortgage loan to buy a condominium. The cost of the condo is $130,000. I will make a 20% down payment on the condo, because I do not want to pay mortgage insurance. The down payment will be $26,000 ($130,000 x .20 = $26,000). That means I will borrow $104,000 ($130,000 - $26,000 = $104,000). The loan term is 30 years. The lowest interest rate I could find was with my neighborhood bank for 5.5%, and this bank had the lowest fees.

$$\$104{,}000 \ \times \ \frac{(1 + .055/12)^{360} \times .055/12}{(1 + .055/12)^{360} - 1} = \$590.50 \text{ Monthly Payment}$$

This means *each month* over a 30 year period, I will have to pay $590.50 for a mortgage loan.

Total Amount Paid for the Loan = Monthly Payment x   n

$212,580 = $590.50 x 360

Total Amount Paid in Interest = Total Amount Paid for the Loan – Principal

$108,580 = $212,580- $104,000

Analysis:

My annual salary, gross income, is $80,000 or $6,666 per month.

      My monthly expenses for "housing" would be: $590.50 mortgage, $250 condo fees, homeowner's insurance $80, property taxes $303 for a grand total of $1,223.50. $1,223.50 is 18.35% of my gross income ($1,223.50 / $6,666 = $1,223.50).

      My monthly expenses for "non-housing" are expected to remain the same for the next 5 years: $277.55 student loan payment. I paid-off my car last year and will choose to drive it for 5 more years. $277.55 is 4.16% of my gross income ($277.55 / $6,666 = .0416).

      My monthly expenses for "other" includes $1,866 income and social security/medicare taxes, $80 car insurance, $100 health insurance, $25 doctor visits and prescriptions, $400 food/groceries, $250 fuel for car, $300 entertainment and dining out, $50 cable, $70 cell phone, $60 water service, $25 trash service, $60 gas service, $60 electricity, $150 clothes and shoes, $50 laundry and dry cleaning for a grand total of $3,546 per month. $3,546 is 53.19% of gross income ($3,546 / $6,666 = .5319).   Based on my circumstances, I feel like I cannot cut my expenses any further.

      Given the above scenario, I will continue my aggressive savings plan to buy nice furniture to last a lifetime, make a down payment for a car to buy in 5 years, take a reasonably priced vacation once each year, put money in my employer's 401k plan, put money in my own IRA, put money in a non-retirement mutual fund account, and put cash in an interest bearing account. I will therefore save 24.3% of my salary, gross income each month. (I reached this number by taking 100% - 18.35% "housing" – 4.16% "non-housing" – 53.19% "other" obligations = 24.3%.) I will keep 4.3% for "other" expenses I do not anticipate each month. So, overall, I will save 20% of my salary each month. Since my gross income is $6,666 per month, if I save 20% of my income, I can save $15,998.40 in one year. After I have saved this money, my first priority is to buy furniture and a laptop computer. I realize if I had taken a credit card loan to buy furniture and a laptop computer costing $8,500, and I paid it off in one year, the interest cost to me, at 20% interest per year, would have been $1,700. By saving in advance, I saved myself $1,700 in credit card interest. (Once you realize how hard it is to save money, you will not want to spend money.)

Because I have already saved enough money to cover one year of "housing," "non-housing," and "other" (taxes and required living expenses) obligations, I feel very confident buying this condo at $130,000. I know I can afford the condo.

NOTE:

You should be aware when shopping for the lowest and best interest rate for loans, financial institutions will quote an interest rate, fixed or variable, and an APR (Annual Percentage Rate). Financial institutions should provide you with both rates, and if they do not, ask. (Today, credit card companies may only quote the APR.) Loan contracts, such as a mortgage contract, will list the interest rate, not the APR. The APR is another way of looking at interest, whether it is fixed or adjustable (variable, changing). The APR is a calculation you can find on FDIC's website, www.fdic.gov, in the document *Determination of Annual Percentage Rate*. FDIC regulates how financial institutions can calculate the APR. The APR is annualized (expressed as a yearly rate), and takes into account the interest rate as well as charges and some fees. For a mortgage loan, fees may include broker fees, extra point fees you can pay to drive down the interest rate, closing costs and other fees. Other personal loans may have loan origination or underwriting fees, broker fees, transaction, settlement, closing costs, or other fees. When evaluating the best deal, I start by looking at the APR, but it doesn't stop there. I look at the interest rate including fees, charges, penalties, and interest rate changes. Since the loan contract states the interest rate, I want to know the interest rate. I want to spend the least amount of money, overall, when taking a loan.

Excel Formulas

On the next page you will find the formulas to use in Excel to calculate *fixed* and *adjustable* interest rate loans. For adjustable interest rate loans, you can only enter the interest rate you know. When the rate changes, re-do the calculations. **The steps to follow include: 1)** Enter the information in Column A **2)** Enter the information in Column C **3)** Enter the formulas in B5, B8, & B11 exactly as is **4)** Finally, enter the known numbers in B1, B2, & B3.

I recommend setting up the formulas and then making sure you get the correct answers based on the Examples in this Table. Always double check and triple check the formulas to ensure accuracy, before running any numbers.

After entering the known numbers in **Step 4**, the answers will appear where the formulas were entered.

Calculating loan payments will be useful throughout your lifetime.

Please go to the Federal Trade Commission's website for the most up to date information on what is identity theft and how to protect yourself from identify theft, www.ftc.gov/idtheft. See **Table 1**, Consumer Protection.

Employers Will Learn Your Personal Financial History

You should know prospective employers can and will do a credit check with one of the credit reporting agencies. This means they will know whether or not you have been responsible in your private life. You can severely limit your chances of getting your ideal job with the employer of your choice if you have been financially irresponsible, even if you have good intentions of paying off your obligations. Employers want to hire responsible employees they can trust to stay within budget constraints, complete assignments on-time and who do not have to worry about their private lives. Paying a bill on-time is like completing an assignment on-time. Living within your means is like operating within a company's departmental budget.

Grades and Test Scores

When you are a Freshman and not later than when you are a Junior in high school, you should begin thinking about which college or university you would like to attend. Look up the admission requirements for the college you would like to attend on the college's website. When making decisions for admissions, colleges may consider high school grade point average (GPA), high school class rank based on GPA, SAT or ACT test scores, and perhaps other requirements or recommendations such as taking specific courses in high school, taking college courses in high school, types of courses taken as a Senior in high school, a written essay, letters of reference, and leadership experience. Some colleges want you to keep track of and report on the number of hours of extracurricular activities and community service you performed while in high school. The entrance requirements for the colleges of your choice and any requirements for scholarships or grants for which you intend to apply, will now become your goals to achieve. This chapter will focus only on grades and test scores.

Test Scores

Colleges will require applicants to take either an SAT or ACT exam and may require a minimum score. You should plan to beat the minimum score if there is one. If there is not a minimum score, you still need a high score in order to be considered for admission to competitive colleges. You should understand how your score compares to the scores earned by other students, also known as percentiles, as provided by the testing organization. Many colleges look at percentiles and provide these statistics on their websites.

During your Sophomore year or the summer between your Sophomore year and Junior year in high school, I would recommend taking an SAT or ACT pre-test study course and purchasing a pre-test study book from a bookstore. You will learn the type of test questions, how to problem solve, and how to take the test to get the best possible score. You should take several practice tests before taking the real test. If you have test anxiety, it helps to take and re-take the practice tests under test conditions. Your score on the practice tests should exceed the entrance requirements by the college of your choice. When you are confident you will score well on the SAT or ACT to exceed the entrance requirements by the college of your choice, schedule and take the test. The test can be scheduled online through www.collegeboard.com for the SAT and www.actstudent.org for the ACT. Take the test during your Junior year in high school allowing plenty of time to spare if you have to re-take the test, although you should not, if you did well on the practice tests. If you do not do well enough to meet the entrance requirements for the colleges of your choice, take the test again before the deadline set by each college for which you are applying. It is up to you to find out when the college application deadline is and by when you must have taken the SAT or ACT for the colleges of your choice. There are rules about the number of times you can re-take the tests and the time required between re-tests. Before you take the test, you should be sure you are going to do well on the test, and this is accomplished by taking and re-taking practice tests through a pre-test study course and through pre-test study books.

Grades

Some colleges have a GPA requirement for admission. If the colleges of your choice and any scholarships for which you intend to apply will accept a high school GPA of no less than 3.7 out of 4.0, then I would recommend setting your target high school grade at 4.0 out of 4.0. That means, you would need to earn an A in each and every class from your Freshman year through Senior year in high school. It is important to have a target or goal that is greater than the application requirements, because it is possible you could miss your target due to an unexpected event or circumstance. That is just a fact of life, and we are human. I would recommend reviewing your GPA at the end of each semester so that you can plan what your grades should be in each class for the next semester in order to exceed the GPA college application requirements. If the college of your choice does not have a GPA requirement or statistics of past admissions, I would focus on competing with yourself to get the highest possible grades. (You may limit your college choices if your GPA is too low. Limiting your college choices may limit your future employment choices.) The goal is for you to have a chance of getting into the college of your choice and getting the scholarships or grants you want. Planning ahead is very important.

Some colleges may require high school graduates to meet a minimum GPA requirement and/or to be ranked in say, the top 10% of their graduating class. That means, if you have a graduating class of 1000 students, your GPA would need to be at most the 100th highest GPA in your graduating class. If your GPA is the 101st highest, then you would *not* meet the top 10% requirement. If your GPA is the 99th highest, then you *would* meet the top 10% requirement in this example. Just as you would monitor your GPA, you would need to monitor your class rank throughout high school. Some high schools do not rank their students, but it is up to you to find out early on by asking your high school counselor.

When you are a Senior in high school, take a course on "How to Study in College." There are many good books on how to study and get good grades as well. One of the common themes is you need to study and do your homework as you go, not cram the night before. I cannot tell you how important this is. You must know how to study when you get to college in order to earn the highest possible grades. Prospective employers want to see high grades.

Depending on the college you attend, course grades may be determined based on a "grading curve." You will find many college courses are graded on a curve, which means only a certain percentage of students in each of your classes will make an A, say 10%. The percentages of A's, B's, C's are predetermined by the instructor or institution. Each student will compete with other students in each course. If you want to earn the highest grade possible, it is important to ask the instructor what the grading system is, if it is not already clearly defined, during the first day of class. The grading system should be documented and distributed to all students. I like to see the "grading curve" system or any grading system for that matter as an opportunity to compete with myself rather than with others. My grade is about me, what I learned, and how accurate I can be when responding to questions. I check and re-check my answers to ensure accuracy. – Think about it. This is exactly what one should do when working for an employer as well. Having the correct information and accurately communicating the information, verbally and in writing, are so very important for success in the working world.

If you decide you do not like an instructor, then you will have to work with it and continue to seek your target grade. I have talked with several college students who told me they would intentionally make a bad grade to show the instructor how bad his lectures are. Know, if the instructor is a bad instructor, most likely he does not care who learns or not; so your cause will be lost. Remember, when you make a bad grade, it reflects poorly on YOU. If you talk about how bad an instructor is, people will think you are making excuses for not committing yourself to the higher grade. You are building your future, and you cannot let a bad instructor negatively impact your future. Consider taking a class from an instructor you do not like as character building. Think about how the instructor could improve and perhaps take it under consideration for any presentations or lectures you yourself might give in the future. Never, ever tell the instructor how he could improve, as a less ethical instructor would let this impact your grade.

I know someone who outright told his English professor she did not know how to teach. This was the last class he needed to get his engineering degree. He did not pass the class and never got his degree, 20 years later. While not getting his degree was his choice, I think this is an important lesson for students.

When you get into the college of your choice, remember grades mean a lot to prospective employers. If your college grades are too low, you may not get the job, career or employer of your choice. When interviewing for a job, prospective employers will ask you what your GPA is. Prospective employers will always ask for your transcript. From an employer's perspective, when applying for post college jobs, you should have an overall and major GPA of 3.25 or greater out of 4.0, have work experience related to the job for which you are applying, and have solid leadership experience to be a *very* desirable job candidate. You will still be considered a desirable candidate with a 3.0 out of 4.0 GPA, related work experience, and solid leadership experience. A GPA of less than 2.8 out of 4.0 may limit your career and employer choices. I cannot stress this enough. Further, if you choose not to work at all during college, and I would advise against this because having related work experience is very important to employers, you will need a very high GPA such as a 3.8 out of 4.0 from a competitive college, and you must have solid leadership experience to be a fairly desirable job candidate. However, keep in mind, those *with* related work experience may trump your *lack of* related work experience.

High School and College Leadership

I cannot tell you how important it is to obtain leadership experience when you are in high school *and* college. Prospective employers want to see solid leadership experience on a resume. Some employers will only hire candidates with leadership experience.

High school and college leadership experience will help set you apart from other candidates. High school leadership experience may help you become admitted to the college of your choice or help you obtain an internship in high school or college with an employer of choice. College leadership experience may help you get a college job, college internship, or full-time job after college as employers will look for those with leadership skills and experience. Getting leadership experience in high school and college benefits you in that it allows you to begin developing your leadership style in a "low risk" environment, meaning you can learn from your mistakes early on without having it affect your career.

What is leadership? Leadership means different things to different people. In general, I would say a leader is someone who inspires people and convinces them to follow him or her to achieve a goal. A political candidate's goal may be to increase voter awareness for himself or herself and to convince voters to vote for him or her. Because the candidate cannot possibly do all the work as there are simply too many potential voters to reach, the candidate must lead a team of people who have assigned tasks to achieve the overall goal, winning the election. A leader will define and communicate the goal, anticipate any hurdles that may prevent the goal from being achieved, set team members up to work well together, ensure team members are assigned to do tasks in areas they are skilled, ensure the team has the "tools" necessary to achieve the goals throughout the project, and facilitate issues in a timely manner to move the project forward and to be completed on time and within budget.

There are many qualities and characteristics of a leader. I will touch on a few here but this is not intended to be all-inclusive. Some of the best leaders are honest, direct, genuine, caring, enabling in a positive way, set organizational/team goals and achieve these goals honestly and on-time, provide honest feedback, admit own mistakes, and want the best for themselves and their team and behave accordingly. All of this means leaders are excellent anticipators and initiators, problem solvers, communicators, and people persons. A people person is someone who talks with team members (not down at them) and helps team members work well together despite their differences. A person who pits people against each other is not a leader and may prevent goals from being achieved or being achieved on-time. Being a people person will set you apart from everyone else. See **Table 1**, Leadership Defined.

When you are in high school, I would recommend joining at least one organization each year to get some participatory membership and leadership experience. Participatory membership experience means you are actively making suggestions and participating on a team to accomplish a goal. This is also very important for developing social skills. Participatory membership experience might be obtained by joining any school or outside organization such as the school newspaper, school yearbook, language club, math club, science club, prom committee, sports team, Girl Scouts, Boys & Girls Club, organizations associated with the YMCA such as Youth and Government and Hi-Y, and others you identify. Leadership experience can be obtained as a student council member, class officer, committee leader/chairperson, club officer, yearbook editor, newspaper editor, team captain, crew leader, community organizer, fundraiser, and many more. Providing community service such as through a volunteer service organization is considered leadership experience as well. See **Table 2**, Volunteer Service Organizations.

When you are in college, I would recommend joining at least two on or off campus organizations and becoming a chairperson, sub-committee leader, director, captain, trainer, community organizer, or other title in which you have the opportunity to lead a group of people to accomplish a goal. Again, there are many volunteer service organizations where you can get leadership experience. See **Table 2**, Volunteer Service Organizations. To make the experience most meaningful to you, you should select an organization whose mission is one you believe in. You

Table 1

Leadership Defined

A leader is one who:

- Defines goals, sets goals, communicates goals, and achieves goals honestly, on-time, and within budget

- Behaves in a manner in which the leader expects team members to behave: honest, direct, values differences, cares about people and the goals, treats team members respectfully, wants everyone to succeed

- Takes the initiative to suggest and/or to make an improvement without being told to do it

- Requires high quality work from herself and from team members

- Inspires people to be their best and to do their best

- Communicates well both verbally and in writing

- Gets people to volunteer to work on specific tasks that are within their skill set (that they are qualified to do)

- Inspires team members to complete their tasks that contribute to the goal (Kicking someone in the backside, metaphorically, is not inspirational to anyone and the extent to which it is carried out often borders on unprofessional behavior.)

- Removes barriers to completion and provides the "tools" needed for team members to complete tasks that contribute to the goal

- Anticipates problems before they happen and removes barriers/sets a different path to ensure the anticipated problems do not become problems

- Solves problems well, keeping in mind the goals and budget of the project, when the unanticipated happens

- Provides honest feedback to each individual on the team, privately (not in front of other people)

- Admits own mistakes

- Is a people person who talks *with* the team and not *at* them, values differences, and encourages teamwork

should also select an organization you can be proud of displaying on your resume. You will have four years to do this, but I recommend you obtain your experience beginning as a Freshman in order to help you obtain college internships or other jobs during college. College internships and other college jobs can help lead to full-time employment after you graduate.

Table 2

Volunteer Service Organizations

<u>High School</u>

Many organizations offer programs for teens to perform community service and gain leadership experience. Joining these organizations is a great way to make friends and network contacts as well. Schools may or may not advertise these programs and therefore, you may need to do an internet search to identify programs in your city. Many of these organizations offer college scholarships, but you have to learn in advance what it takes to win a scholarship and set those requirements as your goals to achieve.

- Habitat for Humanity. Habitat for Humanity builds affordable housing in the U.S. and abroad. Habitat offers programs for those aged 14 – 25. Through Habitat, you can organize and participate in educational and fundraising activities, and you can help build a house if you are at least 16 years of age.

  www.habitat.org/youthprograms/int/

- Interact by Rotary International. Rotary International has an international humanitarian focus such as health, population growth, environmental issues, poverty, and literacy. Interact is designed for those aged 14 – 18.

  www.rotary.org/en/StudentsAndYouth/YouthPrograms/Interact/Pages/ridef ault.aspx

  www.rotary.org/en/AboutUs/SiteTools/ClubLocator/Pages/ridefault.aspx

- Junior Optimist Octagon International (JOOI) by the Optimist Club. "By providing hope and positive vision, Optimists bring out the best in kids" is the mission of the Optimist Club. JOOI provides programs in which kids help kids.

  www.optimist.org/default.cfm?content=vistors/vis3.htm

  www.optimist.org/countrydirectory.cfm

- Key Club by Kiwanis International. Kiwanis performs community service activities. Key Club is for high school students.

  www.kiwanis.org/

  www.keyclub.org/

- Leo Club by Lions Club. Lions Club is a community service organization.

  www.lionsclubs.org/EN/content/youth_leo_clubs.shtml#

- Exchange Club. The Exchange Club is a community service organization.
  www.nationalexchangeclub.org
  www.nationalexchangeclub.org/findclub/weblocator.asp
- Your Local Food Bank and Other Local Community Service Organizations.

College

- Circle K International (CKI) by Kiwanis International. Kiwanis performs community service activities with a focus on children. CKI is for college students.
  www.kiwanis.org/
  www.circlek.org/
- Habitat for Humanity. Habitat for Humanity builds affordable housing in the U.S. and abroad. Habitat offers programs for those aged 14 – 25. Through Habitat, you can help build a house, and you can organize and participate in educational and fundraising activities.
  www.habitat.org/youthprograms/int/
- Jaycees. The Jaycees is an organization providing community service and is designed for those aged 18 – 40.
  www.usjaycees.org/
  www.usjaycees.org/index.php?option=com_mtree&task=listcats&cat_id=95&Itemid=177
- Rotoract by Rotary International. Rotary International has an international humanitarian focus such as health, population growth, environmental issues, poverty, disability, and literacy. Rotoract is designed for those aged 18 – 30.
  www.rotary.org/en/StudentsAndYouth/YouthPrograms/Rotaract/Pages/ridefault.aspx
  www.rotary.org/en/AboutUs/SiteTools/ClubLocator/Pages/ridefault.aspx
- Exchange Club. The Exchange Club is a community service organization.
  www.nationalexchangeclub.org
  www.nationalexchangeclub.org/findclub/weblocator.asp
- Your Local Hospital. Many local hospitals have a Community Service and Volunteer Service organization. I anticipate a strong need for college and graduate students with health-related degrees for volunteer work and unpaid internships.
- Your Local Food Bank and Other Local Community Service Organizations

Take notes on your leadership experience as it occurs such as who, what, where, when, why, and to what extent so that you can transfer important information to your resume. You should be sure to state your leadership experience and the goals you accomplished on your resume, as prospective employers will search out this information. If you do not list your accomplishments on a resume, you may have a difficult time getting interviews. Once you have the interview, be prepared to talk about your leadership experience.

Meaningful Work Experience in High School and College

While I have already mentioned the need to obtain meaningful work experience, I have included it as its own chapter, because it is so very important for getting a good first job after graduating from college. Potential employers will review your resume and ask if you have any related work experience to the position for which you are applying. In most cases, a new college graduate will say "no." This is where I want you to be a step ahead of everyone else and be different.

You need to obtain work experience related to your career interest while in high school *and* during your college years, whether it is a paid or unpaid internship, unpaid volunteer at a non-profit organization, part-time job, summer job, or Co-op job. A Co-op job is usually one in which a college student alternates between completing a semester of college and completing a semester of work for an employer for an agreed upon time period. Some co-op jobs allow you to work part-time while attending college. Co-op jobs can be applied for through College Career Centers or directly on some employer websites. Please refer to the chapter on "College Career Centers." The Cooperative Education & Internship Association has a search directory of co-op coordinators at specific colleges which you might find useful, www.ceiainc.org/directory.asp?PageID=261. However, if you do not see your college, please call your college's Career Center.

A couple of years ago, I toured the Jamestown Settlement in Virginia. Our tour guide was a man in his late 20's, who told us he had worked as an intern at the Jamestown Settlement when he was in *high school*. During his internship, he was very fortunate to unearth an artifact of significance and said he was "hooked" on archaeology ever since. He went all the way and got his PhD in archaeology and returned to continue his work at the Jamestown Settlement.

Employers hiring entry-level employees right out of college almost always require the person to have some job experience related to the open position. Obtaining an internship while you are in college is a good way to get experience. Both paid and unpaid internships can be applied for through College Career Centers and online with specific employers for which you are interested in working. To find prospective employers, you can look through the phone book or through an online directory. To find websites for specific employers, you can simply google the name of the employer, go to the employer's website, and find the career/job webpage, which is sometimes buried in the "About us" section. I recommend trying to obtain a college internship with a company you would like to work for in a full-time capacity after graduation. That way, you and the employer have a chance to try each other out.

If you are lucky enough your college internship could become your full-time career when you graduate. A friend of mine is an artist. For many years she has offered a student internship through a local university. Students apply for the internship which offers an opportunity to learn about the fine art business and to receive college credit. As a benefit, the internist gets to see the world during school breaks. The last internist worked out so well, my friend hired her full-time when she graduated and even purchased a condo for her to live. Now, that is a once in a lifetime opportunity. My friend's internist told me, she found the work she loves, an employer she loves, and she grabbed a great opportunity to live out her dreams.

A good way to get some relevant work experience in college is through a required internship which earns you college credit. A required internship is part of the study curriculum and is sponsored by the school (i.e. business, engineering, liberal arts) within the college you attend. Required internships are not offered for all majors and at all colleges. As with any college internship, I would not rely on one internship to be your sole experience, unless it is rather lengthy, covering about 1 - 2 years.

Another friend of mine completed her required internship for the Master of Public Health program. Following her internship after graduation, she was offered a more responsible position by the same employer.

While these are all good examples, you cannot count on being hired full-time by your internship or co-op employer. Not all employers are able to hire full-time workers in the same department. Be sure to ask during the internship or co-op interview process if the company or department has a history of hiring their interns or co-ops after graduation. Asking the question should open the conversation so you can begin to understand if the company is planning to hire you, if you do well. However, I want to be clear, regardless of what the company says, you should not count on the company to hire you. Things happen. Be sure to apply for full-time jobs with other employers during your Senior year of college.

What You Need to Know Before Selecting a College

Selecting a college can be very difficult. However, there are some things you need to consider when selecting a college, such as graduation rates, cost of tuition, acceptability by employers, credit transfer to another college, acceptance of CLEP, acceptance of AP courses, and having an assigned academic advisor. While this sounds overwhelming, it is fairly easy to research. These considerations are designed to help you get the most out of your college education and value for your money.

As a first step, go to the National Center for Education Statistics' website to review survey data, http://nces.ed.gov/ipeds, including graduation rates and tuition of specific colleges and universities. Another website using the same data but may be more pleasing to the eyes is www.collegeresults.org by The Education Trust, Inc. Both websites allow you to compare multiple colleges.

Use the above websites to find the four-year, five-year and six-year graduation rates for all of the colleges you are considering, including your nearest state university and colleges of adults you know who have good, well-paying jobs. Harvard University sets the standard high with a six-year graduation rate of 98% in 2008. The University of Texas at Austin had a six-year graduation rate of 77.8% in 2008. Arizona State University had a 56% six-year graduation rate in 2008.

Importantly, when you are on the above websites, you need to compare the cost of tuition and fees at the colleges you are considering.

As a second step, verify the college is recognized and acceptable by reputable employers in your career field. You need to do this before attending any college. A college education without recognition and acceptance from reputable employers has very little value. -- Is the college well-recognized by employers in your career field?

To find the answer to this question, go to websites of employers you would like to work for. Look at the leadership and employee profiles and find where they went to college. Look at the employer's recruiting or employment webpage to find from which colleges they recruit and for which positions. Does the employer recruit at your desired college in your career field? If you know working adults in your career field, ask them which colleges they would recommend and not recommend based on their experience.

You need to also find out if the college has a Career Center. If so, which employers have returned at least three (3) years consecutively to recruit at the institution? For which specific positions did they hire each year? This information should be published on the college's website in some form or a handout should be provided to you. Word of mouth is not good enough. A true career center is one in which a student can apply for internships, co-op jobs, part-time jobs, full-time jobs during college, and full-time jobs after college graduation. A true career center will also help you write a resume and prepare for interviews by conducting mock interviews. A true career center will have staff whom are dedicated to helping students find jobs and get jobs in their preferred career fields.

Thirdly, there must be credit transferability to other colleges. This question holds true for any college.

If you decide after one or two semesters you do not like the college for whatever reason, or if you plan to go to a community college first and then transfer to a four year university, can you transfer your credits to your local state university or other university of interest? To answer this question, you will need to contact directly the colleges or universities of interest to you to ensure they will accept college credit from the college you plan to attend. Get this in writing. Be sure you do this check before you start any college or you could end up taking the same courses again and consequently paying twice, if you choose to transfer colleges.

As a fourth step, ask the college or university if it accepts CLEP (College Level Examination Program) by the College Board. In other words, you want to find out if you can take a test to forego taking lower level college courses. You can do this in a number of subjects including mathematics and languages. Be sure to find out in advance how many courses/credits the college accepts through CLEP and which subjects are acceptable. Also, get this in writing. The cost of taking the test is far less than the cost of tuition for one class.

As a fifth step, if you took AP (Advanced Placement) courses in high school, ask the college or university if it provides credit and/or advanced placement for achieving specified scores on the AP College Board exam, for the courses you took. The college sets a limit on the number of courses/credits you can receive. Get all of this in writing before you decide which college to attend. Again, the cost of taking an AP exam is far less than the cost of tuition for one class.

Finally, ask the college if you will have an assigned academic advisor. You definitely want someone watching out for you.

To help you start organizing your thoughts *before* completing the College, Career, and Money Plan worksheet at the end of this book, try completing the below chart. You can easily set-up a comparison spreadsheet like this in Excel and add more colleges.

College Comparison Chart

	Name of College	Name of College	Name of College
Graduation Rate			
4 Year			
5 Year			
6 Year			
Cost of Tuition and Fees			
Acceptable by Employers in My Field. My Field of Interest is _____.			
Does the College Have a Career Center?			
Do Employers I prefer Recruit at the College?			
Do These Employers Recruit in My Field of Interest?			
Will I Be Able to Transfer Credit to This College			
Name of College			
Name of College			
Name of College			
Name of College			
Accepts CLEP			
Courses Accepted			
Max. Number of Credits/Courses Accepted			
Accepts AP			
Courses Accepted			
Max. Number of Credits/Courses Accepted			
Will I have an assigned Academic Advisor?			

College Career Centers

The College Career Center, or other name as appropriate for the college, serves as a clearinghouse for employers seeking college students and college students seeking employment opportunities. Through the Career Center, college students apply and interview for summer jobs, part-time jobs, internships, co-op jobs, and full-time work related to the degree. In addition, the Career Center should offer help for writing resumes and preparing for job interviews.

Career Centers can be campus-wide or by school (i.e. business, communications, liberal arts, engineering). You will need to build a relationship with someone in the office to learn about advertised and unadvertised opportunities at the earliest time possible so you can be considered for any interviews. Find out at the beginning of each semester or quarter when resume reviews and interviews will be scheduled. This is easy if the system is online. If your college will allow it, you should begin submitting your resume for specific positions at least eight or nine months prior to when you want to start working. For example, if you will graduate in May, you should begin applying for specific positions in early September or the earliest possible time as appropriate for your college.

Not every college has a Career Center, and it is up to you to discover whether the college of your choice has one before applying for admission. (Please see the previous chapter, "What You Need to Know Before Selecting a College.") Many employers use Career Centers to recruit new college graduates with limited experience and may not advertise for these positions on their company websites. In addition, many employers recruit at select colleges for specific positions. For example, Company A recruits at Universities 1, 2, and 3 for marketing positions only and recruits at Universities 4, 5, 6, and 7 for engineering positions only. Employers tend to recruit in parts of the country where they are based or where they have an office. Employers who are based in the Midwest tend to recruit from colleges in the Midwest. If you want to live in the Southwestern part of the United States when you graduate from college, it might be a good idea to find a college in the Southwest. I would recommend reviewing the college's website or contacting the Career Center of the college of your choice to understand which companies recruit at the college, for which positions, and for which locations. Some employer websites now provide information on college recruitment including where they recruit, but may not advertise for which positions, and in that case, you can contact the recruiter if the name is provided on the website.

Placement statistics are also very important. Some competitive colleges keep statistics on the percentage of graduates placed within a certain period of time upon graduation. If the college does not display statistics on its website, then there is a good chance the college does not keep statistics or the results are not worthy of displaying on the website.

Have your resume and interviewing skills ready. Many Career Centers will assist you with building a resume and conducting mock interviews. I would recommend finding out if the college of your choice offers these services as it is important support for the college student who wants a good start in life.

Finally, the Career Center is only one avenue for finding work related to your career plan. Other options for finding work include networking, calling targeted employers, applying for jobs on specific company websites, websites for Honor Societies of which you are a member, and websites for professional or trade organizations of which you are a member.

Selecting an Employer Right for You

To increase your chances of longevity with an employer, you will want to select an employer that has the same values and ethics as you do.

Values have to do with the number of hours employees are expected to work whether it is 40 hours per week or 80 hours per week, employee promotion policy and opportunities for advancement, vacation policy, healthcare benefits, retirement plans, number of hours employees are expected to provide volunteer services per year, percentage of salary employees are expected to donate to charities, level of integrity and professionalism, employee learning and collaboration, free training provided to employees, full reimbursement for business expenses, reimbursement for college tuition for a higher degree, and others.

Ethics has to do with how a business and its employees arrive at making decisions. The decisions might be the benefits packages offered to employees, how employees are treated, how customers are treated, how vendors and contractors are treated, if quality issues are addressed, and how financial results are reported. It is very difficult to know this before working for an employer. However, reach out to your network of trustworthy people you know, such as family, friends and neighbors for anyone who has personally worked for or done business with this employer to learn about the company's practices. (I would not rely on second hand information as this is nothing more than gossip and the information may not be factual.) Another way you can learn about a company's ethical practices is through conducting an internet search and reading articles online. (Everything you read online is not necessarily true and therefore you have to consider the source of the information. The *Wall Street Journal* would be considered a credible source as compared to say an unknown news blog that does not have a formal system for verifying information.) You can also learn something about the company through the interview process. Consider each one of these resources when making a decision about a company.

If you research and then interview with a company and tell yourself you could work there for a year or two, then that tells me you believe the company is not the best fit for you. Hopefully you will be able to find an employer who you think is totally awesome, and you would consider staying there a while, as that is in YOUR best interest. Prospective employers will always look at the number of times you changed employers when considering you for a position. If you are 30 years old and have worked for 10 employers, your resume may be overlooked, as there will be those who are as qualified and may have worked for only one or three employers in positions of increasing responsibility. In the eyes of an employer, longevity shows the ability to work with people, commitment to your work, and success in your work such that you were promoted.

I talked with a young woman who was completing her thesis in Organizational Psychology and was interviewing for consulting positions. She said she interviewed for a full-time position with a company that did not ask her any questions about herself. She arrived for the interview and the firm immediately asked her to sign a contract without talking with her first to find-out if she was a fit for the position and the company. She did not sign anything, left the "interview" and did not accept the offer. She was very smart. Any company who does not disclose information about themselves and who does not ask recruits to disclose information about themselves is a potential problem waiting to happen.

References

Throughout high school, college, and your professional career, you should have a list of ready references to help you get admitted to the college of your choice, obtain a job, join a club or organization, or serve on a committee or board. These references should be people who can speak highly of your character and qualifications. References can be personal, academic, and business. Personal references include adult friends of the family who know you well, neighbors who know you well, and school/college administrators who you have regular contact with. Academic references include your high school teachers or college professors. Business references include colleagues and bosses.

Prospective schools and employers may want to contact your references directly rather than receiving a reference letter. Before giving contact information, be sure to contact your reference first to make sure it is okay to use him/her as a reference. This is a courtesy. Any surprise phone calls to your reference could work against you. Be sure to stay in contact with your reference, if only once a year, if you expect to use the reference again and for any networking purposes in the future. Plus, it is always nice to have another friend. Successful people I know have stayed in contact with their references and other colleagues for more than 20 years.

While in high school, I worked part-time in a bank. The Vice President of the bank was kind enough to tell me I could use him as a reference when I graduated. When I applied for a job during college, my prospective employer contacted my reference. My reference had very kind words for me, and I was hired. The lesson here is your reference can help you get a job.

Networking

As I mentioned previously, I founded a large organizational networking group with a previous employer about 16 years ago to help improve business results through personal and professional development. In this case, we can look at networking as a tool to help you get the career you want. Are you ready?

What is Networking?

The goal of networking is to exchange information with someone you know or someone you do not know in order to receive a desired outcome, or benefit, for both parties. For example, the desired outcome for you might be learning unadvertised information concerning a job in which you are interested that could lead to an interview for the job and consequently lead to your getting the job. The desired outcome for the person you are talking with might be having the satisfaction of helping a young person get her first job out of college. As another example, you may seek information from an adult in a career of interest to you. The benefit to you is that you will gain an understanding of potential career paths for your ideal and ultimate job. The benefit to the adult is he will have the satisfaction of helping a young person prepare for the future.

Networking can be a very powerful tool when it comes to learning about degrees you need for the career you want, careers and career paths, learning about unadvertised job openings, and learning good information you need to know in order to be successful in school and at work.

When you are in college and are trying to get your first job, you definitely take more than you give, because you have been focusing on growing-up and studying in school. When you are in college, it is very easy to meet people in class, at campus events, and at campus organization meetings. However, it is very important to meet people who have full-time work in the field you are interested in working. Join reputable organizations on campus or off-campus where you can meet people who have full-time work in your field(s) of interest.

In college, I volunteered with a campus organization to help escort a U.S. Foreign Service Officer to a campus event at which he was speaking. I picked him up at the airport, took him to his hotel, took him on a campus tour, watched his presentation, and took him back to the airport. As is a common question to ask college students, he asked me what I wanted to do when I graduated. Quite frankly, I was not sure, but I knew I wanted to help people and perhaps do something internationally. He told me if I wanted to become a Foreign Service Officer, he would be happy to recommend books to read in preparation for the exam. He gave me his business card and told me to call any time if I wanted help. I appreciated that very much. While I did not take him up on his offer for more information, the opportunity was there. The same opportunity can happen to you.

Career Path Networking

Below is a checklist of questions designed to help you complete part of the College, Career, and Money Plan worksheet. These are recommended questions for talking with someone who is an expert in your field and position of interest. I would recommend 1) talking with a Human Resources Manager or Director in a company of interest to you and then 2) talking with a Director or Vice President responsible for the field or position of interest to you. (If you want to be a Product Development Engineer, you would talk with a Director or VP of Product Development.)

✓ How long have you worked in your field or industry? (The field or industry might be healthcare, consumer products manufacturing, product development, regulatory affairs, customer service, marketing, sales, aerospace engineering, petroleum engineering, human resources, information technology, supply chain, geology.)

✓ What is it like working in your field or industry? What is the culture? What are the values? What are your company's values? What issues are facing the industry?

✓ What do you like about the field or industry? What do you dislike?

✓ How long have you worked for your company? What do you like about your company?

✓ If my ideal and ultimate job is _____, what would be a possible career path? What type of jobs would you recommend for high school and college that would help me get my first real job after college? Is the career path you mentioned valid for most companies or does it vary? What are the job titles and responsibility levels within your company for each job on the career path? What are the number of years one can expect to be in each job on the career path? How much money does one make in today's dollars for each job on the career path? What are the skills required for each job along the career path?

✓ What does it take to get promoted within your company?

✓ What degree(s) and any certification(s), license(s), or registration(s) do I need in order to obtain my ideal and ultimate job as well as the other jobs on the career path?

✓ Based on my ideal and ultimate job, does it matter from which college I get my degree(s)? (Some industries and employers like to hire for specific degrees from specific colleges.)

✓ Be sure to ask any other questions that might be helpful for you. Remember, this is your life.

When networking with those in the working world, it is important to make the best possible impression, as you never know if there might be a potential job opportunity for you in the future. I would recommend scheduling the meeting for no more than 20 minutes, in which case you will need to be brief and do a lot of listening. You will need to be professional, which means arriving on time for your meeting or making your call as scheduled, not exceeding your scheduled meeting time unless the person indicates it is okay, organizing your thoughts before your meeting, asking good follow-up questions as needed, completing any follow-ups to your meeting as you committed, and writing a formal "thank you" letter. Be sure to take good notes when talking with each person so that you can complete part of your College, Career, and Money Plan worksheet. The nice thing about this type of networking is that it allows you to further develop your professionalism skills, speaking skills, social skills, note-taking skills, and letter writing skills. You might even learn about internship or other job opportunities if you are lucky.

Example of Career Path Networking

In this networking scenario, I am a young high school student who wants to learn about a career in hospital administration. I reviewed everything I know about careers in hospital administration online. Now, I am pretty sure this is what I want to do for a living, and I am ready to investigate further. At my high school's career fair, I talked with several healthcare professionals representing several hospitals at the fair about the type of work involved in healthcare administration. I learned some information but not enough information to develop a possible career path as well as information about length of service in each position and potential salaries. At the career fair, I asked several of the hospital representatives if they could refer me to someone who could provide me with information about a possible career path, etc. All of the hospital representatives I asked said they could not refer me to someone because what if all of the students wanted referrals. My next step was to think about who I would know or my parents would know that could help me answer my questions. I remembered one of our neighbors is a nurse. Great! I asked my parents if it was okay if I contacted her with my career questions. My parents offered to go with me to ask questions, and I let them. We knocked on our nurse neighbor's door and explained what information I wanted. She said she would make some phone calls and see who at her hospital could help me answer my questions. Two days later, our nurse neighbor called me at home and told me the Director of Human Resources and Vice President of Operations agreed to talk with me. I called the Director of Human Resources first. She talked about some potential career paths, because there is not just one way of achieving a hospital executive position with her hospital. She talked about salary ranges for each position on the career paths. Then she said the number of years in each position was entirely up to the person in the position, how well the person performed on the job, and the positions that become available. I thanked her, and then I called the Vice President of Operations. I explained to the Vice President of Operations the information I was looking for and why. She asked me what the Director of Human Resources had told me and confirmed it was accurate. Then she told me if I was interested in a hospital administration executive position, my undergraduate degree should be science-related such as nursing, and I should get an MBA with a concentration in Finance. She encouraged me to work for about three to five years in nursing to understand the dynamics of nursing and then to apply to MBA school, as most MBA schools require work experience. She encouraged me while working on my MBA, to intern at a hospital in administration. I should start applying for administrative positions at least six (6) months prior to graduating with my MBA. Within the first few months after graduating with an MBA and I am in my new hospital administration position, I should apply for an Administrative Fellowship at various hospitals. An Administrative Fellowship is essentially an executive-in-training program that typically lasts for one year. An Administrative Fellowship can help me move up faster in the organization but is not guaranteed because there are very few positions available. She stated that career paths were very dynamic and changing because of many factors such as fit with job, how well the person performs, and which positions are available and when. The Vice President of Operations stated this was her advice but encouraged me to talk with others. She did not have anyone she could refer me to. At this point, I felt like I had enough information to develop a preliminary career path.

Networking Is Not About Gossiping

Networking is not a tool to be used for initiating or spreading gossip. Remember, networking is about sharing information that benefits both parties. Gossip usually only benefits one person, the teller, and usually has some form of fiction inserted into the teller's scenario, and the teller most certainly would not want the target to know from where the information came. You must always question the motivations of a person who persistently gossips, makes negative personal statements about many individuals. Networking is an opportunity to better yourself and the person with whom you are talking. Serious companies want to remove gossips, not hire them.

Your Resume

You will need to have an updated resume throughout high school, college, and your professional career. It is a good idea to keep copies of the resumes you produced throughout your lifetime for reference, in order to help you better recall information that is on, say, an old resume, rather than your latest resume, should you forget. Trust me, this happens! I would not want you to forget how brilliant you were 10, 20, 30 or even 40 years before!

In general, a resume should include any honors received, your overall grade point average and major grade point average, organizations of which you are a member and can be proud of, leadership positions held (i.e. captain, project leader, director), paid and unpaid jobs held that are relevant to the type of work you are seeking, results achieved through any project you started and finished. Be sure to use action language that shows you did not need someone to hold your hand the entire time to get the work done, that you have initiative and the ability to follow-through on your commitments. Use language like "developed," "created," "led," "sold," etc. Finally, list your strengths (what you are good at doing). Have a friend, parent, or experienced counselor review your resume for typos, formatting advice, and any suggestions. When you are in college, the College Career Center should help review your resume as well as provide mock interviews.

At the end of this chapter, you will find a sample resume each for high school, college, professional career up to five years after college, and professional career six years or more after college. The purpose is for you to see how a resume evolves over time for one person. The professional career resume allows you to see

Resume Checklist

The following should be included on any resume throughout high school, college, and your professional career, unless otherwise indicated. Please note: when applying for professional jobs after college, you do not need to include high school information unless it is relevant to the type of position you are applying, and it most definitely adds value to your resume.

- ✓ Overall GPA (high school & college resumes, up to five years after college)
- ✓ Major GPA (college resume, up to five years after college)
- ✓ Honors received such as honor society memberships, Dean's list (high school & college resumes, up to five years after college)
- ✓ Special honors and appointments such as a Fulbright Scholar
- ✓ Organization memberships of which you are proud to display on your resume
- ✓ Leadership positions held either at work, as a volunteer, or at school
- ✓ Paid and unpaid jobs relevant to the type of work seeking
- ✓ Results achieved through any project you started and finished
- ✓ List of your strengths (what you are good at doing) such as written and/or verbal communications, creativity, leadership, analytical skills, organization skills, quality-oriented, customer-oriented, language skills, technical skills related to the job for which you are applying. When you list your strengths, you should be sure the rest of your resume reflects your strengths. For example, if under "Strengths," on your resume, you list "Written Communications," then your "Work History" or "Organization Activity" should indicate what exactly you did that reflects being an excellent written communicator, such as writing a monthly report or selling an article to a local newspaper.

a career path in addition to a detailed description of the work performed for each position on the career path.

When you are in high school, college, and the early years of your professional career, your resume should only be one page. When you have more years of experience, say 15 years, your resume should not exceed two pages.

Your resume should be customized for each position for which you are applying. By doing this, it takes more time to apply for positions, but it gets better results. For example, if Position A requires specific experience as a developer of web content, and Position B does not require experience as a developer of web content, then you should include your experience as a developer of web content for Position

A, and you do not necessarily have to include the specific experience on your resume for Position B unless you think it will help you get the job. One of the reasons for doing this is that a resume with a lot of irrelevant information (in the eyes of the specific recruiter) may get overlooked as the resume may simply have way too much information on it. This becomes a bigger problem for professionals with a lot of experience but is worth mentioning to help you focus your resume on the job you want.

This page is intentionally left blank.

YOUR NAME

Sample –
High School Resume

1XX Apple Street
Austin, Texas 78705
512.222.XXXX Cell
yourname@comcast.net

CAREER OBJECTIVE:

Your Name seeks a position as a 2012 Summer Intern in grant-writing with an overall career objective to work in fundraising development.

EDUCATION:

Fall 2011

Senior, River High School
Current GPA: 3.8 out of 4.0
National Honor Society member

> Every person is different and has different backgrounds, skills, goals, and accomplishments.

WORK HISTORY:

Summer 2010

Intern, St. Peter's Health System Foundation
- Developed a prospective donor database of 10,000 names. Analyzed database software and made recommendation on which software to use.
- Awarded certificate of achievement for "Best Quality Work"

ORGANIZATION ACTIVITY:

Summer 2011

Habitat for Humanity
- Assisted with building a house in Venezuela. Served as translator.

2009 - 2010

President, Spanish Club
- Organized and led club meetings
- Suggested and organized first attempted fundraiser, raising $10,000. Spoke at event with 100 people in attendance.

2003 – Current Girl Scouts
- Suggested and organized first attempted Holiday Dinner for the elderly in 2009
- Sold more Girl Scout cookies than any other Girl Scout in Texas in 2007 and 2008
- Earned 100% of all possible badges

STRENGTHS:

Leadership, Organization, Quality-Oriented, Verbal Communication, Analytical Skills, Fluent Spanish

> You can set goals for yourself to gain experience in the Strengths (i.e. Leadership, Organization, Communication) you want to build-on, while working toward your career goals/objectives. Once you have the experience, then you can place it on your resume.

YOUR NAME

Sample –
High School Resume

1XX Apple Street
Austin, Texas 78705
512.222.XXXX Cell
yourname@comcast.net

CAREER OBJECTIVE:

Your Name seeks a position as a 2012 Summer Intern in grant-writing with an overall career objective to work in fundraising development.

EDUCATION:

Fall 2011   Senior, River High School
                   Current GPA: 3.8 out of 4.0

[Quality-Oriented]   National Honor Society member

WORK HISTORY:

Summer 2010   **Intern**, St. Peter's Health System Foundation   [Analytical Skills]
                   - Developed a prospective donor database of 10,000 names. Analyzed
                     database software and made recommendation on which software to use.

[Quality-Oriented]   - Awarded certificate of achievement for "Best Quality Work"

ORGANIZATION ACTIVITY:

[Fluent Spanish, Leadership (Participating in positive social change vs. leading a group of people)]

Summer 2011   Habitat for Humanity
                   - Assisted with building a house in Venezuela. Served as translator.

2009 - 2010   President, Spanish Club   [Leadership (Leading a group of people), Organization, Verbal Communication]
                   - Organized and led club meetings
                   - Suggested and organized first attempted fundraiser, raising $10,000.
                     Spoke at event with 100 people in attendance.

2003 – Current Girl Scouts
                   - Suggested and organized first attempted Holiday Dinner for the elderly in
                     2009

[Leadership, Organization]   - Sold more Girl Scout cookies than any other Girl Scout in Texas in 2007 and
                     2008
                   - Earned 100% of all possible badges

STRENGTHS: [Follow-through is not listed as a Strength, but it is important to show on a resume that you can start and finish something with success]

Leadership, Organization, Quality-Oriented, Verbal Communication, Analytical Skills, Fluent Spanish

Strengths are listed at the bottom of this resume. At least one example of each Strength is provided on the resume.

YOUR NAME

Sample –
College Resume
(Before graduation)

2XX Jackson
Chicago, IL 60610
312.444.XXXX Cell
yourname@comcast.net

CAREER OBJECTIVE:

Your Name seeks a half-time position as a grant proposal writer with an overall career objective to work in fundraising development.

EDUCATION:

Fall 2013

Sophomore
University of Illinois at Chicago
Major: Management
Minor: Marketing, Sociology
Overall GPA: 3.8 / 4.0
Major GPA: 4.0 / 4.0
Dean's List, Spring 2013

You can set goals for yourself to gain experience in the Strengths (i.e. Leadership, Organization, Communication) you want to build-on, while working toward your career goals/objectives. Once you have the experience, then you can place it on your resume.

WORK HISTORY:

Summer 2013

Intern, America's Second Harvest, Chicago, Illinois
- Wrote grant proposals to foundations and corporations. Met with foundation managers. Secured $25,000 in grant funding.
- Analyzed and summarized grant reports in a written report and made an oral presentation to management

Summer 2012

Intern, America's Second Harvest, Chicago, Illinois
- Analyzed and summarized grant reports in a written report and made an oral presentation to management

Summer 2010

Intern, St. Peter's Health System Foundation, Austin, Texas
- Developed a prospective donor database of 10,000 names. Analyzed database software and made recommendation on which software to use.
- Awarded certificate of achievement for "Best Quality Work"

ORGANIZATION ACTIVITY:

Winter Break 2012

Rotoract
- Assisted with installing a water tank and making service connections to 100 households in Panama. Served as translator.

Fall 2012 –
Spring 2013

American Marketing Association, UIC Student Chapter
- President
- Suggested and organized first attempted fundraiser, raising $10,000 to send student members to the annual meeting.

Summer 2011

Habitat for Humanity
- Assisted with building a house in Venezuela. Served as translator.

STRENGTHS:
Leadership, Organization, Quality-Oriented, Communication, Analytical Skills, Fluent Spanish

YOUR NAME

Sample –
College Resume
(Before graduation)

2XX Jackson
Chicago, IL 60610
312.444.XXXX Cell
yourname@comcast.net

CAREER OBJECTIVE:

Your Name seeks a half-time position as a grant proposal writer with an overall career objective to work in fundraising development.

EDUCATION:

Fall 2013

Quality-Oriented

Sophomore
University of Illinois at Chicago
Major: Management
Minor: Marketing, Sociology
Overall GPA: 3.8 / 4.0
Major GPA: 4.0 / 4.0
Dean's List, Spring 2013

Strengths are listed at the bottom of this resume. At least one example of each Strength is provided on the resume.

WORK HISTORY:

Summer 2013

Written and verbal communication, Follow-up and Follow-through to completion

Intern, America's Second Harvest, Chicago, Illinois
- Wrote grant proposals to foundations and corporations. Met with foundation managers. Secured $25,000 in grant funding.
- Analyzed and summarized grant reports in a written report and made an oral presentation to management

Analytical Skills

Summer 2012

Analytical Skills

Intern, America's Second Harvest, Chicago, Illinois
- Analyzed and summarized grant reports in a written report and made an oral presentation to management

Leadership (Made Recommendation)

Summer 2010

Quality-Oriented

Intern, St. Peter's Health System Foundation, Austin, Texas
- Developed a prospective donor database of 10,000 names. Analyzed database software and made recommendation on which software to use.
- Awarded certificate of achievement for "Best Quality Work"

ORGANIZATION ACTIVITY:

Fluent Spanish, Leadership (Participating in positive social change vs. leading a group of people)

Winter Break 2012

Leadership (Leading a group of people, initiative and follow-through), Organization

Rotoract
- Assisted with installing a water tank and making service connections to 100 households in Panama. Served as translator.

American Marketing Association, UIC Student Chapter
- President

Leadership (Title Only)

- Suggested and organized first attempted fundraiser, raising $10,000 to send student members to the annual meeting.

Summer 2011

Habitat for Humanity
- Assisted with building a house in Venezuela. Served as translator.

Fluent Spanish, Leadership (Participating in positive social change vs. leading a group of people)

STRENGTHS:
Leadership, Organization, Quality-Oriented, Communication, Analytical Skills, Fluent Spanish

BERNTZEN

YOUR NAME

Sample –
Professional Resume
(Up to five years after college
graduation)

1XX La Salle
Chicago, IL 60610
312.444.XXXX Cell
yourname@comcast.net

CAREER OBJECTIVE:

Your Name seeks a full-time position as a Fundraising Development Manager.

EDUCATION:

2016
BS Management, University of Illinois at Chicago
Overall GPA: 3.75 / 4.0
Major GPA: 4.0 / 4.0
Dean's List, Beta Gamma Sigma Honor Society

GPA and honors are
listed on a resume up
to five years after
college graduation.

WORK HISTORY:

2016 – 2018
Analyst, Fundraising Development, America's Second Harvest,
  Chicago, IL
- Wrote grant proposals to foundations and corporations. Met with
  foundation managers. Secured $800,000 - $1 million in grant funding.

Summer 2015
Intern, America's Second Harvest, Chicago, IL
- Wrote grant proposals to foundations and corporations. Met with
  foundation managers. Secured $80,000 in grant funding.

Summer 2013
Intern, America's Second Harvest, Chicago, IL
- Wrote grant proposals to foundations and corporations. Met with
  foundation managers. Secured $25,000 in grant funding.
- Analyzed and summarized grant reports in a written report and made an
  oral presentation to management

Summer 2012
Intern, America's Second Harvest, Chicago, IL
- Analyzed and summarized grant reports in a written report and made an
  oral presentation to management

ORGANIZATION ACTIVITY:

2017 - 2018
Rotary International
- Assisted with building a water filtration system in Bangladesh during a
  two week vacation.

STRENGTHS:

Leadership, Organization, Quality-Oriented, Verbal and Written Communications, Analytical Skills,
Fluent Spanish

INTERESTS:

Reading, Current Events, Community Service, Softball, Skiing

YOUR NAME

Sample –
Professional Resume
(Six or more years after
college)

1XX La Salle
Chicago, IL 60610
312.444.XXXX Cell
yourname@comcast.net

EXECUTIVE SUMMARY:

Well-rounded professional with more than fifteen (15) years of fundraising development experience.

EDUCATION:

Can you identify the lifetime Career Path for this person? See the answer on a duplicate copy of this resume.

2021   MBA, Depaul University, Chicago, IL
2016   BS Management, University of Illinois at Chicago

WORK HISTORY:

2028 – Present   **Vice President, Development Services,** National Council of YMCAs   of the USA, Chicago, IL
- Develop strategic plan and balanced scorecard with the team. Direct fund-raising program.
- Raised $80 million in 2028, $92 million in 2029, $105.8 million in 2030
- Exceeded fund-raising goal by 15% each year
- Develop and manage operations budget of $1.5 million
- Manage staff of 15
- Serve on Board of Directors. Provide reports and speak on behalf of the organization.

2022 – 2028   **Director, Development Services**, National Council of YMCAs of the USA, Chicago, IL
- Implemented fundraising program with the team
- Provided input to strategic plan
- Raised $30 million in 2027
- Exceeded fund-raising goal by 15% each year
- Initiated the development of 12 new sponsors over six year period
- Managed operations budget of $400,000
- Managed staff of 5
- Developed weekly written report
- Served as speaker at fundraising events and programs
- Suggested and initiated the development of a donor appreciation program, implemented in 2023

2018 – 2022   **Manager, Fundraising Development**, America's Second Harvest, Chicago, IL
- Wrote grant proposals to foundations and corporations. Met with foundation managers. Secured between $1.5 – $ 6 million per year in grant funding.
- Suggested, researched, and developed a customer survey for 200-member food banks. Analyzed the data using statistical analysis. Developed a written report and made an oral presentation to management.

YOUR NAME

1XX La Salle
Chicago, IL 60610
312.444.XXXX Cell
yourname@comcast.net

| 2016 – 2018 | **Analyst, Fundraising Development**, America's Second Harvest, Chicago, IL |
| | - Wrote grant proposals to foundations and corporations. Met with foundation managers. Secured $800,000 - $1 million in grant funding. |

| Summer 2015 | **Intern**, America's Second Harvest, Chicago, IL |
| | - Wrote grant proposals to foundations and corporations. Met with foundation managers. Secured $80,000 in grant funding. |

Summer 2013	**Intern**, America's Second Harvest, Chicago, IL
	- Wrote grant proposals to foundations and corporations. Met with foundation managers. Secured $25,000 in grant funding.
	- Analyzed and summarized grant reports in a written report and made an oral presentation to management

| Summer 2012 | **Intern**, America's Second Harvest, Chicago, IL |
| | - Analyzed and summarized grant reports in a written report and made an oral presentation to management |

ORGANIZATION ACTIVITY:

| 2025 - 2027 | Habitat for Humanity |
| | - Assisted with building a house in Aurora, IL during a one week vacation. Served as Spanish translator as needed. |

| 2020 – 2022 | President, American Marketing Association, Chicago Chapter |

| 2017 - 2018 | Rotary International |
| | - Assisted with building a water filtration system in Bangladesh during a two week vacation. |

STRENGTHS:

Leadership, Organization, Quality-Oriented, Verbal and Written Communications, Analytical Skills, Fluent Spanish

INTERESTS:

Reading, Current Events, Community Service, Softball, Skiing

YOUR NAME

1XX La Salle
Chicago, IL 60610
312.444.XXXX Cell
yourname@comcast.net

EXECUTIVE SUMMA This resume is a bit simplified, but it gets the point across.

Well-rounded professional with more than fifteen (15) years of fundraising development experience.

EDUCATION:

Notice increasing levels of responsibilities through the years.

2021	MBA, Depaul University, Chicago, IL
2016	BS Management, University of Illinois at Chicago

WORK HISTORY:

2028 – Present

Specific examples of Strengths are captured on the resume.

Vice President, Development Services, National Council of YMCAs   of the USA, Chicago, IL
- Develop strategic plan and balanced scorecard with the team. Direct fund-raising program.
- Raised $80 million in 2028, $92 million in 2029, $105.8 million in 2030
- Exceeded fund-raising goal by 15% each year
- Develop and manage operations budget of $1.5 million
- Manage staff of 15
- Serve on Board of Directors. Provide reports and speak on behalf of the organization.

2022 – 2028

Notice the MBA was earned one year before the person was promoted to a Director level position. Without an MBA, this person may not have been able to obtain a Director level position.

Director, Development Services, National Council of YMCAs of the USA, Chicago, IL
- Implemented fundraising program with the team
- Provided input to strategic plan
- Raised $30 million in 2027
- Exceeded fund-raising goal by 15% each year
- Initiated the development of 12 new sponsors over six year period
- Managed operations budget of $400,000
- Managed staff of 5
- Developed weekly written report
- Served as speaker at fundraising events and programs
- Suggested and initiated the development of a donor appreciation program, implemented in 2023

Manager, Fundraising Development, America's Second Harvest, Chicago, IL
- Wrote grant proposals to foundations and corporations. Met with foundation managers. Secured between $1.5 – $ 6 million per year in grant funding.
- Suggested, researched, and developed a customer survey for 200-member food banks. Analyzed the data using statistical analysis. Developed a written report and made an oral presentation to management.

YOUR NAME

1XX La Salle
Chicago, IL 60610
312.444.XXXX Cell
yourname@comcast.net

2016 – 2018	**Analyst, Fundraising Development**, America's Second Harvest, Chicago, IL
	- Wrote grant proposals to foundations and corporations. Met with foundation managers. Secured $800,000 - $1 million in grant funding.
Summer 2015	**Intern**, America's Second Harvest, Chicago, IL
	- Wrote grant proposals to foundations and corporations. Met with foundation managers. Secured $80,000 in grant funding.
Summer 2013	**Intern**, America's Second Harvest, Chicago, IL
	- Wrote grant proposals to foundations and corporations. Met with foundation managers. Secured $25,000 in grant funding.
	- Analyzed and summarized grant reports in a written report and made an oral presentation to management
Summer 2012	**Intern**, America's Second Harvest, Chicago, IL
	- Analyzed and summarized grant reports in a written report and made an oral presentation to management

ORGANIZATION ACTIVITY:

2025 - 2027	Habitat for Humanity
	- Assisted with building a house in Aurora, IL during a one week vacation. Served as Spanish translator as needed.
2020 – 2022	President, American Marketing Association, Chicago Chapter
2017 - 2018	Rotary International
	- Assisted with building a water filtration system in Bangladesh during a two week vacation.

STRENGTHS:

Leadership, Organization, Quality-Oriented, Verbal and Written Communications, Analytical Skills, Fluent Spanish

INTERESTS:

Reading, Current Events, Community Service, Softball, Skiing

The lifetime Career Path for this person is:
Intern
Intern
Intern
Analyst, Fundraising Development
Manager, Fundraising Development
Director, Development Services
Vice President, Development Services

Part III

Making Decisions for Today and Your Future

Making decisions are a part of everyday life. We must decide whether to get out of bed, when to get out of bed, when to arrive at school or work, whether to do quality work or just get by, whether to learn or not. What you decide today can impact your tomorrow and your long term future. You will also impact the lives of your friends and family through the decisions you make.

Understand the Consequences of Your Actions

Understanding the consequences of what you do, say, and don't do is a solid step toward maturity. You should understand the message you are sending to others *before* you do it, say it, or don't do it. Acting responsibly is solely your decision.

If you want people to think you are caring and responsible, as an example, you can demonstrate this by arriving on-time, doing what you said you were going to do no matter how small or large the task by when you said you were going to do it, and with quality. The benefit of doing what you said you were going to do is that you will become reliable and trustworthy to others. This is an excellent trait to have in the real world.

If you arrive late and do not accomplish what you said you were going to accomplish habitually, or the quality of your work is frequently poor, then people may think you are uncaring and irresponsible. This is true of any person at any age. I know this is not you, because you are showing an interest in self improvement by reading this book!

Deciding to be good with money is a terrific decision for anyone, because it can bring peace of mind and stability not only to you but to your family. If you have not read the chapter on "Money for College, Money for Life" yet, I ask you to read it, because having money and access to money is very important for feeling secure and building a life that is comfortable for you.

As another example of understanding the consequences of your actions, examine the choice between driving under the influence of alcohol and not. Before you say, "Oh, I've heard that before," please hear me out. I would like to share this story with you, because it is so important and demonstrates the example I want to provide. When I was a high school student, I would go with a friend and her parents to their ranch on occasional weekends. My friend and I got to know many local teens in this rural area. As I recall, three local teens were driving back home after a night in another small town. The driver was intoxicated and had two friends in the car. Their car was driving at a high rate of speed on the interstate and hit an 18 wheeler that was parked on the shoulder. These friends had many choices that night. The choices they made ended their lives and impacted the lives of their families and friends forever. It has been almost 30 years, and I still remember.

While reality shows can be entertaining to watch, recognize real life is different from a reality show. Reality shows have fabricated environments and game rules. These game rules are different from society's rules. Society, including businesses, has rules, such as exhibiting manners and being kind and respectful to people. In the real world, we follow society's rules. Just know, because someone on a reality show says something or does something, it does not mean you, personally, should say it or do it in real life. Again, a reality show is different from real life.

Be careful about comments you make online, such as on blogs and social media. While these are great forums, these are not forums to express every thought you have and every action you take to every human being on earth. Parents, teachers, friends, enemies, and employers will all find your site, one way or another. Anything you say, whether you are joking or not, can come back to haunt you, including school suspension, not being able to hang out with the friends you want, not getting the job you want, and even job loss once you have a job. Think twice before you publish your thoughts and actions to the world. A good rule of thumb is, if you hesitate to publish something, please don't publish it. I want you to be successful.

There are many different scenarios in which what you do, say, and don't do will impact you and other people. You should be aware of the benefit or harm you will cause by doing it, saying it, or not doing it.

Do the right thing

Oftentimes doing what is easy seems like the right thing to do, but in the end it can harm us and others rather than benefit us. An example of this might be cheating on exams. While the benefit to you if you cheat is you make an A, the harm is you really did not learn anything or learned very little to benefit an employer and the employer's customers. Would you want to go to a doctor who had cheated throughout medical school? Would you want to hire and would you trust an aeronautical engineer to design your planes if you knew this person had cheated on engineering exams?

Sometimes people will ask you to cause harm to yourself and/or other people. It is easy to go along with what other people want you to do. However, I ask you to look at it from this perspective. People may ask you to do anything from being mean to someone, stealing something, or helping someone cheat on an exam. Being mean to someone may harm the person to whom you are being mean, physically or mentally, and temporarily or permanently. However, in the end, being mean to someone can cause harm to you, either through school and college suspensions/dismissals, grounding, lawsuits, jail time depending on the type of harm caused, or you yourself can become a target. Stealing something may bring instant gratification, but I guarantee you, you will be caught eventually. Stealing can result in school and college suspensions, grounding, jail time, fines, lawsuits, becoming an outcast. Helping someone cheat on an exam brings consequences as well. You can be grounded, suspended/dismissed from school and college, and prevented from getting your degree. Please consider any action you are asked to take, not just from these examples, and ask yourself if it causes harm to you or to someone else. If it causes harm to you or to someone else, then it is probably not the right thing to do. Only you can decide.

I hope you will understand the consequences of your actions in advance and choose to do the right thing as you see it, as the decisions you make today can impact your future and perhaps the future of others.

Life Lessons

I have many life lessons I would like to share with you. There are lessons you learn through the experience of other people, and there are lessons you learn on your own. This chapter is intended to help you with the former, so you can know what to expect in life and be a step ahead of everyone else.

I have often said consulting is the ultimate lesson in human psychology. I have worked with people from all backgrounds, and I have worked with employees at all levels in a company from clerks to senior executives. What I learned is everybody is similar, yet we are different. I like the differences because it makes life more interesting and from a business perspective produces powerful business results. I hope you will embrace the similarities and the differences.

Everybody Has Challenges

Everybody has challenges. When I say challenges, I mean, everybody has something they are trying to overcome such as a bad experience, a health problem, a disability, a fear, a need to learn more about a subject. Sometimes challenges are visible and sometimes challenges are not visible. Sometimes people talk about their challenges, and sometimes they do not. Everybody has challenges just as you do.

Accept that People are Different from You

How wonderful it is to go to a party, be in a classroom, or sit around a conference table and have each person be different from me and from each other. That is what makes life interesting and dynamic and from a business perspective, competitive. I have found each person has his or her own specialization in a subject area, has a different background, challenges, education, skills, and goals. It would be very difficult to find two people who are exactly alike.

You will hear a lot about "diversity" when you enter the corporate world. Oftentimes diversity is discussed in terms of race, ethnicity, national origin or ancestry. However, diversity holds a much wider circle for me which includes all differences such as race, ethnicity, national origin, ancestry, education level attained, job title and responsibilities, what state(s) the person was born and raised, religion, age, economic status, disability, challenges, and quite simply anything else that marks us as different from each other, whether the differences are visible or invisible.

When you accept that people are different from you, and they will know by how you treat them, then most likely you will open doors for yourself throughout your lifetime. I have seen this time and time again. Accepting that people are different from you means treating people with respect and dignity. You do not have to agree with what a person is saying, but it is important to treat people with respect and dignity.

Respect

Everyone will have a different definition of what respect means to them, but it usually centers around treating someone in a non-offensive manner. For me, it is being kind, helpful, friendly, truthful, professional, following through on commitments that impact me and in particular when it comes to my time and my money. In return, people may treat you as well as you treat them. The reward for treating people well and in a non-offensive manner is not only living in harmony, but it improves the chances that your business and personal goals will be met.

I know someone who is well-liked by everyone. Throughout his 20 year career he has had opportunities come to him, I believe, because of who he is, how he treats people, and the business results he gets. When he was in his latter twenties, he was working on a project for his company. Each day he made a point to talk with people on the project to hear what they had to say. He did this because he liked people, and he found he learned a lot about the business from talking with people. One day the Project Secretary asked him if she could give his name to her husband who worked for a competing firm. Her husband's firm was looking to hire for a position in another state for a very large project. She said she wanted to refer him because she thought he was a very bright young man, and he took the time to talk with her, unlike the other engineers on the project. It turns out, he eventually took a higher level position with the competing firm, and he has achieved success way beyond where he ever expected to go. It is clear his relationship with this Project Secretary changed his life, and he is grateful to her.

Life is Difficult

Life is difficult, for everyone. The decisions you make throughout your lifetime can impact how difficult your life will be, and sometimes your life will be difficult due to unexpected events which do not have anything to do with you or your decisions.

Your decisions can make life easier or more difficult. For example, if you choose to go to a less reputable college with no or few companies recruiting at that college, then that decision can make it very difficult to get the job and career you planned for. Conversely, if you go to a well-known and highly ranked college in your degree area, and there are many quality employers recruiting at that college for your specialty, then getting a job in the career you planned for may be less difficult, providing you have the grades, related work experience, and leadership experience. If you choose not to be good with money, then your life will be very difficult in particular if you struggle to make payments or have creditors, companies you owe money to who are trying to collect payment, calling you at home and at work. Conversely, if you choose to be good with money, you can feel more secure and focus on living, rather than focus on making payments.

Sometimes an unexpected event happens over which you have no control, such as divorce, an illness or death of a loved one, or the company you work for decides to eliminate your department, including your job! In these cases, it does not mean you did anything wrong. This is life, and life happens to everyone.

Disappointment

Throughout your life, you will be disappointed. Everyone gets disappointed whether they admit it to others or not. It is a fact of life. If you have very high standards, you will be disappointed more often than those who have lower standards. There are times when people will disappoint you, or your failure to achieve a goal, such as not getting into the college you want, not getting the job you want, or not getting the raise you need will disappoint you. In the past, when I have been disappointed, in order to overcome my disappointment, I acknowledged it, I either stayed with the goal or changed the goal if I could control it, and above all, I stayed positive. Thinking good, positive thoughts are most productive for achieving goals, rather than dwelling on the negative. Quite simply, thinking positively gives us hope and allows us to see a positive future. We all need hope, whether we are 13 or 93.

Support Network

We all need a good support network (system – not to be confused with "networking") of close family, friends, and colleagues to talk with, laugh with, just listen, advise us, or encourage us in good times and bad. Having a good support network of people who care about you and you care about them is important to have throughout your lifetime. It is good for your family life and career, and it is good for your physical and mental health. We all need someone to talk with, regardless of age.

Friends

Throughout your life, you will have acquaintances, friends, and life-long friends. Acquaintances are people you see on occasion such as at school or parties, and you may exchange information with them, but you do not know very much about their backgrounds. Friends are people who you know well and exchange information with, and you can depend on for certain things, such as having a good laugh or taking the friend to school or work when her car is in the repair shop. Life-long friends are those who you can tell anything to, and they will still love you.

When it comes to the number of acquaintances, friends, and life-long friends, everyone is different. Some people have few life-long friends, few friends, and lots of acquaintances. Some people have few life-long friends, many friends and many acquaintances, etc. As you go through life, you have to accept what level of friendship people are willing to give you. Conversely, people will have to accept what level of friendship you are willing to give them. This usually works itself out.

Know your childhood and college friends most likely will become your friends and life-long friends. Most importantly, you should surround yourself with people who have the same values, ethics, self-confidence, and who want to make positive contributions to society just as you do. Your friends and life-long friends may go to work in the public, private, non-profit sectors, may work in the U.S. or abroad, and work in any industry. My college friends are from all over the country and the world, have varying majors and degrees, and work in many different fields and industries. – Everybody is different; so your portfolio of friends will be different.

Bullies

This section is for those of you who are being bullied or have been bullied; or perhaps you are the bully, and you do not know it yet. What is a bully? A bully *intentionally* and *repetitively* spreads rumors about people that are not true, verbally abuses people such as hurling insults, physically abuses people, excludes people from groups, and otherwise targets people to try to mentally or physically harm them.[12] Bullies may do this in person or online, called cyberbullying. Some bullies may appear to be popular and likeable people at first glance. Bullies may act alone or with a group of people to attack their target.[12] First, you must know that bullying is caused by psychological factors in the bully. If a person is bullying you, most likely the person is bullying others. Bullying is a repetitive pattern of behavior. If you think you have been bullied or if you think you might be perceived as a bully, to learn more, please go to these three websites: www.stopbullying.gov, http://www.stopbullying.gov/teens/index.html, and www.ncpc.org/cyberbullying.

You should also know, not only are there child bullies, but adults can be bullies as well. Adults may bully kids or adults. Adult bullies lurk in neighborhoods, schools, organizations, at work, and other places where a person might frequent. Adult bullies tend to operate in the same way as child bullies. These adult bullies will try hard to humiliate the target, damage the reputation of the target, and may damage relationships with people who do not know the target well. Adult bullies are found out eventually. In my experience, companies that tolerate these bullies tend to be less effective and less competitive.

Just know child and adult bullies are out there, and just because they bully you, it does not mean you did anything wrong. In fact, most likely these bullies are bullying others, no matter the socioeconomic status of the targets.

If you are ever tempted to bully someone just know you could subject yourself to a lawsuit where you or your parents would have to pay the victim a large sum of money that most likely you or your parents cannot afford, school suspension or dismissal, jail time depending on what happened, becoming an outcast, and ultimately destroying your own future. Please be aware of the consequences of your actions.

If you have been bullied as a child, I want to give you hope. A person very close to me was repeatedly bullied in elementary school. Fortunately for her, her family moved to a different school district, and she was able to make good life-long friends. While she still thinks about it from time to time as triggered by something she sees, today she is a successful senior executive with a large corporation.

If you have been a victim of a crime, I want to give you hope. A friend of mine was assaulted when she was in elementary school. She does think about this every now and then as well, but today she is a successful medical doctor.

No matter what happens to you, you can overcome it. Sometimes you may need help from family, friends, school principals, teachers, counselors, or a school psychologist to talk through what happened and to give you tools to move forward with life. Know it is okay to ask for help. It is healthy to ask for help. You are never alone. Any person who makes you feel like you did something to deserve the bullying is not well-trained, and I would recommend talking with someone else. If you have been bullied, I encourage you to read more about bullying at www.stopbullying.gov, and I encourage you to share this website with an adult family member.

Tomorrow Is A New Day

As a consultant, I worked on many complex projects with some tough characters. Many years ago, I performed an assessment at a manufacturing plant where there was only one female manager. I saw the struggles she went through over a several day period. One day she asked me how I did it. How was I able to work with mostly men in my field? I told her two things: 1) I did not see myself as being the only female. I saw myself as part of the team. Seeing myself as the only female would cause changes to my behavior that would most likely produce an undesirable effect on the team. 2) No matter what happened today, tomorrow was a new day. Carrying around the weight of yesterday, only weighs me down today. In other words, I cannot perform my best if I am thinking about what happened yesterday. I had to learn to let go of events that did not impact my goal, which was to improve performance of the plant. (Of course, you can apply this to your personal and school lives.) I had a client comment once that he did not understand how I could arrive at work with a smile on my face each day knowing what happened the day before. When he said that, I knew I was in the groove. I thank him for that.

The lessons learned were threefold. No matter how different you are, whether you are the only female, the only male, the only one without a PhD, the only teenager, only person of your race, religion, or heritage, or whatever the visible or invisible difference might be, you must see yourself as part of the team contributing toward a common goal. When you do, people will most likely see you as part of the team as well. You must pull your weight as a team member contributing what you can within your skill set. Sometimes it takes team members a while to accept people who they do not know well or who are different from them. If you exclude yourself, others will most likely exclude you or treat you differently. Therefore you must see yourself as part of the team. Second, you must learn to let go of unimportant matters. Third, when you let go of the past, you will see tomorrow as a new day, and you can focus on your goals.

Learn How to Communicate

You will hear throughout your life that communication is important for success. This is very true. If you want to be an outstanding engineer, doctor, historian, teacher, reporter, internal auditor, economic analyst, nurse, manager, director, senior executive, you must be able to communicate well.

Who is an excellent communicator? You are an excellent communicator if you can articulate both verbally and in writing what you want to say in an acceptable and non-offensive manner that advises the appropriate people of your thoughts, intentions, or actions in a timely manner. A good communicator will also listen to what others have to say and take any action as appropriate. Communication is about getting the point across to others both verbally and in writing in a timely manner, and communication is about listening.

A friend of mine is an executive for a large corporation. Throughout her career, her biggest complaint about the job skills of some of the people in her organization has been they do not know how to write letters, reports and other documents well. She has said it is difficult to promote someone who does not have good writing skills. This is your chance to be a step ahead of everyone else.

Appropriate timing of your communication is important. If you tell your boss you are taking a one week vacation the day before the vacation, this would be considered poor communication because the vacation was not communicated in advance according to company policy. If you tell your team today a new project will begin tomorrow, this is poor communication as well as poor planning and will result in poor followership. Everyone likes advance notice for activities that affect them.

Listening is very important for good communication. If you plan a project, any project, without talking with the people who are affected by the project, before the project begins, you risk project failure. Many young managers think they have all the answers and therefore tell project team members what to do, without listening to or allowing team members to talk about their concerns. The problem is, if these young managers had just asked for each team member's input, listened, and incorporated the relevant input into the project plan, the project would have been successful. Again, this is where I want you to be a step ahead, and it is wonderful if you can learn this in high school, as it will benefit you throughout your lifetime.

Let me give you a simple example. Early on a Saturday morning I decided I wanted to sell lemonade that day. I did not tell my brother or parents what I wanted to do. As far as I knew, the family did not have any plans for the day. However, I did not ask. I saw a package of lemonade in the cabinet and thought I could use it. Then I decided I wanted to start selling lemonade at 11:00. At 10:30, I went to make the lemonade but found my brother had mixed the lemonade and had already drunk one quarter of it! While I was asking my brother why he decided to make lemonade just then, at 10:35, my parents told us we were going to go swimming at noon. What happened? In this example, I failed to talk with my parents and brother. If I had talked with them they would have learned I wanted to sell lemonade, and I would have learned what they had planned for the day. They might have asked that I sell lemonade next Saturday. Or, they might have offered to buy more lemonade packets, make a sign, make cookies to go with the lemonade, or to help me in any other way I needed. Wow! In the corporate world, this is the kind of communication and cooperation you want.

Initiative

If you are reading this book, you definitely have initiative. To take initiative means you have the ability to start something, to move forward toward a goal. The goal could be as simple as offering to order and pick-up pizza for everyone in your family, organizing a soccer team, or taking control of your life by planning for the future.

Having initiative is terrific, but you must have follow-through as well. If you start something, then you must finish it. Important for leaders, only start what you know you can finish.

Taking initiative during college is important. Involve yourself on a specific project for a campus organization or a business. Offer your ideas on how to achieve a goal. The goal might be to raise money for an organization, bring a political candidate to campus, increase organization membership, increase sales, improve the efficiency of a program or system, or develop a website. Volunteer to head-up the program or parts of it. Then, lead the work, enlist help from other team members, and achieve your team's goal. This is something that will look very strong on a resume. It shows creativity, initiative, ability to finish something, as well as leadership.

Tips for Better Communication

1. Learn the basics of communication. Be able to communicate with anyone at any employment level (clerk or senior executive), both orally and in writing. If you do not know how to write a sentence correctly and how to write a letter, your job choices throughout life will be limited. Having limited job choices means your earning potential will be limited. I recommend taking several writing classes in high school and college to improve your writing skills. In addition, you will need to be able to express yourself clearly through speaking so that the person on the receiving end will not misperceive what you are saying. Taking several speech or debate classes in high school and college will help improve your speaking skills. When you are talking with a group of people, gauge how well you are communicating. If everyone in a group says "What did you say?" then say it again, but use different words. You must be able to get your point across, and you will, with practice.

2. Read from a book and newspaper every day. Reading exposes you to truth, drama, comedy, fiction and gives you something to talk about at school, parties, work, and events. Reading allows you to keep your vocabulary current, build your vocabulary, and to expose yourself to new styles of writing. Reading allows you to see other points of view and develop your own point of view. Then you can exchange your thoughts and ideas with other people. In addition, reading about current events in newspapers educates you and the more you know, the better decisions you can make for today and your future. For newspapers, I recommend reading your local paper as it is important to know what is happening in your community and any or all of these papers: the *Wall Street Journal*, *Financial Times*, *USA Today*, *Washington Post*, and *New York Times*. Many newspapers are available in your public library and are available online with limited news. If you can read these papers now and gain an understanding of what is happening in the world, you will be a step ahead. Please be patient, because reading and understanding current events takes time. Even if you do not understand it now, keep reading because one day it will click. When you get to college, your professors will recommend additional newspapers, depending on the subject being taught.

3. Never assume you know what a person is thinking, even if you are trained on body language. If you want to know what someone is thinking, ask the individual. Some very ineffective managers rely on their own perceived "thoughts" and perceived "body language" of the individual to determine what a person is thinking and may use this fluffy data to make decisions. (This is also known as "mind-reading.") Serious companies rely on facts, not fluff.

When you are working in a job, whether in high school, college, or as a degreed professional, it is important to have initiative in order to be promoted. You will need to volunteer to take on additional responsibilities in order to build skills and experience that will help you get the next job on your career path. For example, Jeff is a Public Relations Analyst and wants to be a Public Relations Manager. He knows a Public Relations Manager in his company speaks at public events on behalf of the company and provides commentary to the press as needed, in addition to providing written press releases. (A company press release might include a written statement about a product recall or information about a new product or anything else that the company wants to communicate to the public. The press release is then issued to the press / news organizations for publication.) As a PR Analyst, Jeff primarily researches and gathers data for company press releases. During a week when Jeff's PR Manager was very busy, Jeff offered to write a press release. Jeff's manager agreed. Jeff submitted the press release to his manager, and his manager thought it was excellent. Over the course of the next few months, Jeff volunteered to write more press releases. His boss thought his press releases were so good, he asked Jeff to write all future press releases. While it was more work for Jeff and was not included in his "job description," Jeff was thrilled to do it, because it was experience he could advertise on his resume, and more importantly it would help him get the next job on his career path, whether with his current employer or another employer.

Be Yourself

Be yourself. Be proud of who you are. We are all interesting, special, different from others, and yet we all have something to contribute toward a common goal, whether the goal is a school, work, or family goal.

The meaning of "be yourself" will be different for everyone. In general, it means to be "real," "true to yourself," and "not put on airs." It can also mean to use your gift, what you are good at doing, when making a first impression on others. "Be yourself" should be taken into the context of being respectful to yourself and others, understanding the consequences of your actions, and doing the right thing.

Throughout the years, my husband's best advice to me has been to "be yourself." My interpretation of this is to: stick with what I know, use my personality, and find the common bond. He tells me this just before I give a big presentation or have an important meeting, and it always seems to work for me. The meaning of "be yourself" will be different for you.

Recognize Others Will Be Better At Something Than You Are

We are all different from each other, and we all bring a different background and skill set. Focus on what you do well and what you want to improve. It is great to see someone as a role model but know you will never be just like they are, because you are you. A role model is someone who has a talent you admire, such as parenting, teaching, analyzing statistics, speaking, writing, presenting, coaching, selling, etc. I always like to ask people who have a talent I admire, how did they get to where they are, and how did they get to be so good at what they do? The response broadens my perspective and helps me develop ideas about the types of behaviors I can develop that will produce desired results within the context of my own background, abilities, and endeavors. In other words, this helps me improve my own skill set in an area where I want to improve. Being jealous of someone who does what I want to do but cannot do at this moment in time, does not benefit me or the other person. In fact, the jealously would become apparent, and it would only make both parties miserable. Accept that others will be better at a skill you desire to be good at doing, make a plan on how you can improve the desired skill, and follow-through on the plan.

Accept Constructive Criticism

Accept constructive criticism. Constructive criticism is feedback that is delivered with respect (non-offensively) and the intention is to help you improve. The best method for improving yourself as a student, professional, and person is to ask for feedback from teachers, co-workers, bosses, and friends, and to accept the feedback graciously, whether good or bad. Asking for feedback and accepting it shows you care. If you do not ask for feedback, chances are you will only hear the negative. When you receive feedback, determine if it is valid and make changes as appropriate. The only way to improve is to be honest with yourself.

Criticism should be delivered respectfully and not in front of other people. You may have to calmly coach the person on the best method for giving you feedback if you do not think it was delivered respectfully the first time. Know that when someone offers to give you feedback, this can be an open door for coaching. Coaching provided by a person you respect could lead to a more powerful you, at any age.

Once you receive constructive feedback, chances are if many people are telling you to improve in the same area, then the suggestion might very well be valid. Look for feedback to be either subtle or direct.

As an example of subtle feedback, I once gave a client an organizer at the end of a project with the hope he would use it. He was a very bright young man in his field. He smiled widely and said he had received two other organizers on his last job!

You should know it is very difficult for someone to give direct, constructive feedback. When you receive direct feedback, just know you are lucky the person is sharing with you how you could improve, build your skills, and be the best you can be. The person cares. If you do not accept the direct feedback and refuse to talk about it, the impression is you do not care. If at first you feel the feedback is not valid, then you must calmly ask for clarification and discuss the facts to understand the person's perception. Of course, the person giving feedback could be wrong, but you must be honest with yourself. No matter what, try to *understand* the person's perspective and re-apply your learnings in the future. This is just life.

Know You Will Make Mistakes

While we all strive to make decisions that will bring the greatest benefit to ourselves and other people, we will make mistakes. I have made plenty of mistakes throughout my lifetime. Everyone has. If you make a mistake, it is best to apologize to someone if that is the case, stop tormenting yourself through the use of negative thoughts, remember what you learned, try not to repeat the mistake, and move forward with your life and goals.

Sick Leave

I was talking with a friend of mine who just completed her graduate degree and started working in her first real job. She is excited by her new health insurance, vacation leave, sick leave, and personal days. That discussion sparked this section in my book. I explained to her that in my observations, among those who get promoted are those who do not take all of their sick leave each and every year. If you are sick, you are sick, and you must take your sick leave. However, there are those who feel they are entitled to take sick days even when they are not sick. If you have the "flu" on Fridays and Mondays or every other Wednesday and you do not have a cough or runny nose when you return to work, people will know you are not sick. Human Resources and the Director of your organization will know who calls-in sick and how frequently. Yes. It is best not to call-in sick if you are not sick, if you want to be promoted to a better position in the future or want to receive the highest possible raise.

If you are sick, you are sick, you must take your sick leave, and that is okay. These people usually feel bad when they are sick and actually want to be at work. Your manager will know you want to be at work by your attitude and the quality work you produce, and in this case, your promotion potential will not be affected.

Prevent from Becoming Sick

Remaining healthy is important so you can feel your best while working toward your personal and professional goals. There are several things you can do to help prevent sickness including: washing your hands, cleaning your house, eating nutritious food, exercising regularly, having an annual medical check-up, and having your teeth cleaned twice per year at the dentist.

According to the Centers for Disease Control and Prevention's website, http://cdc.gov/cleanhands, to help prevent you from getting or spreading the cold, flu, or other contagious (infectious) illness, be sure to wash your hands vigorously for 20 seconds with soap and water after going to the restroom, after assisting a child or adult with going to the restroom, after blowing your nose, after tending to a scrape or open wound, after touching blood, after handling animals and animal waste, before preparing food, and before eating. When you are in a public restroom, it is a good idea to use a paper towel to turn off the water and open the door so that you do not re-contaminate your hands. I would also recommend washing your hands when you get home after being out of the home, and washing your hands before touching your face. The reason is, bodily fluids carry germs that can make you or other people sick. Some people do not wash their hands, and therefore what they touch becomes infectious for a period of time, from several hours to several days. Washing your hands with soap and water or using hand sanitizer is a good start for preventing the spread of germs and illness. While you do not want to go overboard with washing your hands, it is important to keep this in mind.

You will also need to clean your home regularly, including bathrooms such as toilets and sinks, kitchens, and surfaces that are touched with the hands such as refrigerator handles, door knobs, cabinet handles, and sink fixtures. It is also important to clean your home after someone in the household has been sick. You will need to use cleansers designed to kill bacteria and common viruses such as the flu virus.

You can help prevent obesity (being grossly overweight), diabetes, and heart disease, all common adult illnesses in the United States, which are *not* contagious like the flu or a cold, by eating well-balanced and nutritious food, by exercising regularly, and by balancing your caloric (calorie) intake with the calories you burn through exercising.

The Centers for Disease Control and Prevention offers information about the basic food groups, www.cdc.gov/nccdphp/dnpa/nutrition/nutrition_for_everyone/basics/food_groups.htm, which is a good start for learning about balanced nutrition. The basic food groups are milk and milk products, meats, fruits, vegetables, grains, and nuts. Another excellent website about nutrition and the basic food groups is www.mypyramid.gov/, published by the Department of Agriculture. Nutrition information is available on the back of food products and is available from many fast food restaurants. The Food and Drug Administration has a great website for learning how to read nutrition labels, www.cfsan.fda.gov/~dms/foodlab.html. You will need to know this information throughout your lifetime, whether you want to prevent from becoming overweight or sick, or whether you are sick and are trying to prevent from becoming sicker.

When you eat food, the body takes in vitamins and other nutrients as well as calories. All serve as fuel for your body. When you are active and exercise, the body burns calories. If you eat more calories than you burn through activity and exercise, then you will gain weight.

There is nothing better than a juicy hamburger, french fries, Tex-Mex food, fried chicken, and Bar-B-Que, all my favorite foods, but I know because of the amount of fat and calories in these foods I love, I cannot eat these foods every day, not even when I was a teenager, because I will gain weight. Foods high in fat have more calories than foods low in fat. I also love foods high in sugar such as crunchy cookies and moist cakes. I know if I eat these foods every day, and I have tried it, I will not get the balanced nutrition my body needs to operate well and help me feel good. Whenever I sit down to a meal, I always consider whether I am including foods from all of the basic food groups and if not, I incorporate what I need in my next meal, as I know that is what my body needs for good nutrition and operation. I consider my body like a machine that needs to be re-fueled with the right kind of fuel in order to keep it in good operating condition.

It is important to be conscious of nutrition and exercise, but it is also important not to carry it to extreme. You need to strike a good balance. You definitely do *not* want to be underweight because if you are, then most likely you are undernourished, and your body can break down. You do *not* want to be overweight or obese because diabetes and heart disease can set-in. Diabetes and heart disease are costly to treat (and quite frankly many people cannot afford the treatment) and both can lead to disability or death. Learning about nutrition and exercise when you are young is important so that you have some control over your own future health. Some things you cannot control, such as if heart disease or diabetes are genetic (run in your family), and some things you can control, such as nutrition and exercise.

If nothing else convinces you to take care of yourself, you can consider the seemingly superficial side. We all want to feel good about how our clothes fit and how we look in our clothes. Also, buying clothes can be very costly, in particular if you go up a size every year of your *adult* life. It would be less expensive to buy fruits and vegetables weekly than to buy a lot of new clothes every year. If you buy good quality, classic (not trendy) clothes for work and you take care of them, these clothes should last for four, five or more years. Yes!

I recommend taking nutrition education and physical education classes in high school, if you are lucky enough to have these classes offered. Regardless, I hope you will go to the three websites listed above to learn all you can about nutrition, and read what you can about diabetes from the American Diabetes Association, www.diabetes.org/, and heart disease and stroke from the American Heart Association, www.americanheart.org/. Finally, to help you stay healthy, you can learn about nutrition and disease prevention on www.healthfinder.gov/, published by the Department of Health and Human Services. Remember, you have a greater chance of achieving your personal and professional goals if you are healthy.

Only Go to College When You Are Ready

I hope you will go to college only when you are ready. If you want to explore life for a year after high school, then do so as your parents will permit. However, I recommend completing and re-evaluating your College, Career, and

Money Plan before mid-term of your Senior year, and in addition, writing down what you hope to accomplish during your break year, how you will pay for your break year, and how your break year will enhance your college application or future job applications. Be aware of college application deadlines, SAT and ACT score dates, any loan application deadlines, and scholarship application deadlines. Some colleges may want you to apply for admission the Summer or Fall *before* you graduate from high school and then apply for a one year "delay" for admission if you get accepted. I personally would feel more secure if I knew I had been accepted to a college before I began my break year. Remember this is your life, every college is different, and it is up to you to find out in advance what the requirements are. Taking a break year is for some people but not for everyone. I hope you will do what is best for you.

Part IV

College, Career, and Money Plan

Reading all of the preceding chapters in this book and conducting your own research through publications, online, and through networking is critical for answering the questions on the College, Career, and Money Plan worksheet. As a high school student, you will need to begin building your resume with leadership and community service experience, work experience, and you will need to know college admission requirements such as high school course requirements, GPA requirements, SAT and ACT score requirements, and many more. You will need to set goals for yourself and work to achieve those goals. Keep in mind, after you complete the College, Career, and Money Plan in high school, you will need to re-evaluate and make changes to it as you see appropriate, once per semester or quarter in high school and college. Once you graduate from college, I recommend re-evaluating and making changes to your plan once per year.

At this point, you may begin completing the College, Career, and Money Plan worksheet for as many ideal and ultimate jobs as you are considering. The worksheet is located at the end of this book, and a completed Example is provided. Completing the worksheet will help you target your career preferences and the colleges to which you apply. Completing the worksheet takes time; so be patient! You might decide to work on it in phases and that is perfectly fine. Take your time. Good luck!

Conclusion

Once you develop a College, Career, and Money Plan, you can be certain it will change over time, as unique opportunities arise, circumstances change, new skills develop, and preferences change.

Always expect the unexpected because life brings uncertainties. It is up to you to anticipate what the unexpected might be. You should have a plan for what you would do if things did not work out with your first preferred college, career, or employer. Keep in mind you will be working so that you and your family will have money to live in the moment and in the future. How well you perform on the job is up to you. How much money you save and spend is up to you.

Some people will excel beyond their wildest dreams. I hope that happens to you. May you be successful in *your* own eyes.

References

1   Bureau of Labor Statistics. *Employment Projections. Education Pays. Education pays in higher earnings and lower unemployment rates.* Retrieved February 16, 2011. http://www.bls.gov/emp/ep_chart_001.htm.

2   U.S. Census Bureau. *Current Population Survey. Annual Social and Economic (ASEC) Supplement. PINC-03. Educational Attainment--People 25 Years Old and Over, by Total Money Earnings in 2009, Work Experience in 2009, Age, Race, Hispanic Origin, and Sex.* Retrieved February 16, 2011. http://www.census.gov/hhes/www/cpstables/032010/perinc/new03_001.htm.

3   U.S. Census Bureau. *Poverty. Poverty Thresholds 2009. Poverty Thresholds for 2009 by Size of Family and Number of Related Children Under 18 Years.* Retrieved February 16, 2011. http://www.census.gov/hhes/www/poverty/data/threshld/thresh09.html.

4   National Association of Realtors®. *Median Sales Price of Existing Single-Family Homes for Metropolitan Areas.* Retrieved February 16, 2011. http://www.realtor.org/wps/wcm/connect/5e37be0045ba291385f5c7342c47dc89/REL10Q4T_rev.pdf?MOD=AJPERES&CACHEID=5e37be0045ba291385f5c7342c47dc89.

5   U.S. Securities and Exchange Commission. *An Introduction to 529 Plans.* Retrieved on February 21, 2011. http://www.sec.gov/investor/pubs/intro529.htm.

6   Internal Revenue Service. *Coverdell Education Savings Accounts.* Retrieved on February 21, 2011. http://www.irs.gov/newsroom/article/0,,id=107636,00.html.

7   U.S. Department of the Treasury. *Education Planning.* Retrieved on February 21, 2011. http://www.treasurydirect.gov/indiv/planning/plan_education.htm.

8   Bureau of Labor Statistics. *Economic News Release. Table 2. Labor force status of persons 16 to 24 years old by school enrollment, educational attainment, sex, race, and Hispanic or Latino ethnicity, October 2009.* Retrieved on February 22, 2011. http://www.bls.gov/news.release/hsgec.t02.htm.

9   U.S. Census Bureau. *Current Population Survey (CPS) Table Creator II (with Customizable Income and Poverty Definitions). Income Definitions.* Retrieved on February 27, 2011. http://www.census.gov/hhes/www/cpstc/apm/incdef.html.

10 Landefeld, J. Steven, Brent R. Moulton, Joel D. Platt, and Shaunda M. Villones. *GDP and Beyond: Measuring Economic Progress and Sustainability.* April 2010. Retrieved on February 27, 2011. http://www.bea.gov/scb/pdf/2010/04%20April/0410_gpd-beyond.pdf.

11 Federal Deposit Insurance Corporation. *FDIC Law, Regulations, Related Acts. 6500 Consumer Protection. Part 226 – Truth in Lending (Regulation Z).* Retrieved on February 28, 2011. http://www.fdic.gov/regulations/laws/rules/6500-1360.html#fdic6500226.14new.

12 U.S. Department of Health and Human Services, Health Resources and Services Administration. *Stop Bullying Now!* Retrieved January 8, 2009. http://stopbullyingnow.hrsa.gov/index.asp?Area=whatbullyingis.

College, Career, and Money Plan Worksheet

NOTE: You are more likely to achieve your goals or near your goals if you have a written plan. WE, as individuals, are constantly evolving and therefore we can change and should change our plan to best suit our needs and interests in high school, college, and throughout our professional careers. It would be unusual for any one person to NOT change their plan at some point in their lives. However, with that said, it is important to have a written plan and work toward your plan's goals. By having a written plan, you are more likely to be successful in achieving your goals or nearing your goals, than if you did not have a plan at all. This plan is for you! Good luck!

Refer to Page #

9   What are your interests?

_____

10   What field or industry do you want to work in?

_____

11   What are your values?

_____

12   Do you have any limitations?
NO!

_____

12, 18   What is your ideal and ultimate job?

_____

12, 13   What specifically do you want to do in your ideal and ultimate job and why?

_____

_____

18   What degree(s) are required to get your ideal and ultimate job? What will be your major or area of concentration?

_____

4   How many years will it take to get each degree? Will you complete all degrees consecutively or will you work for a number of years between each degree? What is your plan?

_____

College, Career, and Money Plan Worksheet

CAREER PATH – What is the expected career path to achieve your ideal and ultimate job?

Refer to Page #	Stage in Life	Expected Job Title	Job Responsibilities	# of Years or Range of Years Expected in Job	$ Expected Annual Salary / Salary Range	Type of Degree and Major Required to Get the Job	Experience and Job Skills Required to Get the Job	Licensures, Registrations, Certifications Required / Recommended to Get the Job, if Any
13 - 20, 101 - 103	**During High School**							
118	H.S. job (related to ideal and ultimate job)							
	H.S. job (related to ideal and ultimate job)							
	During College							
	College job (related to ideal and ultimate job)							
	College job (related to ideal and ultimate job)							
	Degreed Professional							
	1st job (related to ideal and ultimate job)							
	2nd job (related to ideal and ultimate job)							
	3rd job (related to ideal and ultimate job)							
	4th job (related to ideal and ultimate job)							
	5th job (related to ideal and ultimate job)							
	6th job (related to ideal and ultimate job)							
	Ideal and ultimate job							

College, Career, and Money Plan Worksheet

COLLEGE CONSIDERATION

The colleges I am considering for my bachelor's degree include:

_____

_____

_____

_____

The colleges I am considering for my master's degree include:

_____

_____

_____

_____

The colleges I am considering for my PhD or other doctoral degree include:

_____

_____

_____

_____

Some colleges are very competitive and therefore you need to apply to many colleges to ensure you will be accepted.

BERNTZEN

College, Career, and Money Plan Worksheet

COLLEGE ADMISSION REQUIREMENTS

Instructions: For each degree and college you are considering, please complete this information. The information can be obtained from the college's website.

Name of College _____

Degree _____

Major or Concentration _____

Application Deadline _____

Scholarship Application Deadline _____

Cost per 2 semesters (in-state or out-of-state Tuition, Fees, Books) _____

Cost per 2 semesters (Living Expenses) _____

Cost of equipment required (i.e. Laptop Computer) _____

Minimum GPA Requirement _____

Entrance Exams Required (i.e. SAT, ACT, GMAT, GRE, LSAT, MCAT) _____

Minimum Entrance Exam Score Required _____

Other Requirements for Admission _____

_____

_____

_____

_____

_____

_____

College, Career, and Money Plan Worksheet

Refer to Page #

CAN I AFFORD MY STUDENT LOANS?

19, 102

What is your Expected *Annual* Salary for your 1st job as a Degreed Professional?

What is your Expected *Monthly* Salary for your 1st job as a Degreed Professional? Hint: Take the Annual Salary and divide by 12 months.

Will you take out any student loans? If yes, what is the total amount you expect to borrow in student loans?

69, 73

From the Table on **Calculating Loan Payments**, what will be your *monthly* student loan payment after you graduate from college?

159 - 162

Using the **Cost of Living Budget**, will you be able to make your *monthly* student loan payments based on the *monthly* salary from your 1st job as a Degreed Professional? In other words, will you have enough money to pay your student loan, pay taxes, pay rent, buy food, etc.?*

*If you will *not* be able to make your monthly student loan payments based on the Cost of Living Budget, then consider going to a less expensive college that can still help you get the career you want or consider a combination of scholarships and working. As a last resort consider changing careers to one that pays more in salary, if you cannot figure out how to get the finances to work.

BERNTZEN

College, Career, and Money Plan Worksheet

Refer to Page #
80

STATE YOUR GOALS TO ACHIEVE

GPA and Test Scores

My target GPA for high school is a _____ out of _____.

Hint: Make your target GPA higher than the minimum GPA requirement for the colleges of your choice.

The Entrance Exam(s) required for undergraduate (bachelor's degree) admissions include(s):

_____

My target Entrance Exam / Test Score is

Hint: Make your target score higher than the minimum score required for the colleges of your choice.

My target GPA for my bachelor's degree is a _____ out of _____.

Hint: Bachelor's degree GPA's should be no less than a 3.0 out of 4.0 in order to be a desirable job candidate.
       A GPA of 3.25 or higher out of 4.0 is preferred in order to be a more desirable job candidate.

The Entrance Exam(s) required for graduate degree (master's, PhD, or other doctoral degree) admissions include(s):

_____

My target Entrance Exam / Test Score is

Hint: Make your target score higher than the minimum score required for the colleges of your choice.

My target GPA for my graduate degree is a _____ out of _____.

Hint: Graduate degree GPA's should be no less than a 3.5 out of 4.0.

College, Career, and Money Plan Worksheet

STATE YOUR GOALS TO ACHIEVE

Leadership

Enter the type of Leadership experience you would like to pursue in high school, college, and as a degreed professional. Once you have the leadership experience, you can advertise it on your resume to help you get the job and the career you want. Leadership should display initiative and follow-through. (You started at your own suggestion and finished something with success.) When will you pursue and accomplish your leadership experience?

Refer to Page #			Year
84	**During High School**		
	High School leadership	_____	_____
	High School leadership	_____	_____
	High School leadership	_____	_____
	High School leadership	_____	_____
	During College		
	College leadership	_____	_____
	College leadership	_____	_____
	College leadership	_____	_____
	College leadership	_____	_____
	Degreed Professional		
	Extracurricular Activity leadership	_____	_____
	Extracurricular Activity leadership	_____	_____
	Extracurricular Activity leadership	_____	_____
	Extracurricular Activity leadership	_____	_____
	Extracurricular Activity leadership	_____	_____

College, Career, and Money Plan Worksheet

STATE YOUR GOALS TO ACHIEVE

Behaviors

Enter two (2) behaviors you want to improve on each year. How will you do it? When will you do it? Go back at the end of each year to see if you accomplished your goal. You can do this throughout your lifetime.

Refer to Page #
120, 123

Behavior	How	Year

College, Career, and Money Plan Worksheet

COLLEGE ADMISSION REQUIREMENTS

Instructions: For each degree and college you are considering, please complete this information. The information can be obtained from the college's website.

Name of College _____

Degree _____

Major or Concentration _____

Application Deadline _____

Scholarship Application Deadline _____

Cost per 2 semesters (in-state or out-of-state Tuition, Fees, Books) _____

Cost per 2 semesters (Living Expenses) _____

Cost of equipment required (i.e. Laptop Computer) _____

Minimum GPA Requirement _____

Entrance Exams Required (i.e. SAT, ACT, GMAT, GRE, LSAT, MCAT) _____

Minimum Entrance Exam Score Required _____

Other Requirements for Admission _____
_____
_____
_____
_____
_____

College, Career, and Money Plan Worksheet

COLLEGE ADMISSION REQUIREMENTS

Instructions: For each degree and college you are considering, please complete this information. The information can be obtained from the college's website.

Name of College _____

Degree _____

Major or Concentration _____

Application Deadline

Scholarship Application Deadline _____

Cost per 2 semesters (in-state or out-of-state Tuition, Fees, Books) _____

Cost per 2 semesters (Living Expenses) _____

Cost of equipment required (i.e. Laptop Computer) _____

Minimum GPA Requirement _____

Entrance Exams Required (i.e. SAT, ACT, GMAT, GRE, LSAT, MCAT) _____

Minimum Entrance Exam Score Required _____

Other Requirements for Admission _____

College, Career, and Money Plan Worksheet

COLLEGE ADMISSION REQUIREMENTS

Instructions: For each degree and college you are considering, please complete this information. The information can be obtained from the college's website.

Name of College

Degree

Major or Concentration

Application Deadline

Scholarship Application Deadline

Cost per 2 semesters (In-state or out-of-state Tuition, Fees, Books)

Cost per 2 semesters (Living Expenses)

Cost of equipment required (i.e. Laptop Computer)

Minimum GPA Requirement

Entrance Exams Required (i.e. SAT, ACT, GMAT, GRE, LSAT, MCAT)

Minimum Entrance Exam Score Required

Other Requirements for Admission

College, Career, and Money Plan Worksheet

COLLEGE ADMISSION REQUIREMENTS

Instructions: For each degree and college you are considering, please complete this information. The information can be obtained from the college's website.

Name of College

Degree

Major or Concentration

Application Deadline

Scholarship Application Deadline

Cost per 2 semesters (in-state or out-of-state Tuition, Fees, Books)

Cost per 2 semesters (Living Expenses)

Cost of equipment required (i.e. Laptop Computer)

Minimum GPA Requirement

Entrance Exams Required (i.e. SAT, ACT, GMAT, GRE, LSAT, MCAT)

Minimum Entrance Exam Score Required

Other Requirements for Admission

College, Career, and Money Plan Worksheet

COLLEGE ADMISSION REQUIREMENTS

Instructions: For each degree and college you are considering, please complete this information. The information can be obtained from the college's website.

Name of College

Degree

Major or Concentration

Application Deadline

Scholarship Application Deadline

Cost per 2 semesters (in-state or out-of-state Tuition, Fees, Books)

Cost per 2 semesters (Living Expenses)

Cost of equipment required (i.e. Laptop Computer)

Minimum GPA Requirement

Entrance Exams Required (i.e. SAT, ACT, GMAT, GRE, LSAT, MCAT)

Minimum Entrance Exam Score Required

Other Requirements for Admission

BERNTZEN

College, Career, and Money Plan Worksheet

COLLEGE ADMISSION REQUIREMENTS

Instructions: For each degree and college you are considering, please complete this information. The information can be obtained from the college's website.

Name of College _____

Degree _____

Major or Concentration _____

Application Deadline _____

Scholarship Application Deadline _____

Cost per 2 semesters (in-state or out-of-state Tuition, Fees, Books) _____

Cost per 2 semesters (Living Expenses) _____

Cost of equipment required (i.e. Laptop Computer) _____

Minimum GPA Requirement _____

Entrance Exams Required (i.e. SAT, ACT, GMAT, GRE, LSAT, MCAT) _____

Minimum Entrance Exam Score Required _____

Other Requirements for Admission _____

_____

_____

_____

_____

_____

College, Career, and Money Plan Worksheet

COLLEGE ADMISSION REQUIREMENTS

Instructions: For each degree and college you are considering, please complete this information. The information can be obtained from the college's website.

Name of College

Degree

Major or Concentration

Application Deadline

Scholarship Application Deadline

Cost per 2 semesters (in-state or out-of-state Tuition, Fees, Books)

Cost per 2 semesters (Living Expenses)

Cost of equipment required (i.e. Laptop Computer)

Minimum GPA Requirement

Entrance Exams Required (i.e. SAT, ACT, GMAT, GRE, LSAT, MCAT)

Minimum Entrance Exam Score Required

Other Requirements for Admission

College, Career, and Money Plan Worksheet

COLLEGE ADMISSION REQUIREMENTS

Instructions: For each degree and college you are considering, please complete this information. The information can be obtained from the college's website.

Name of College _____

Degree _____

Major or Concentration _____

Application Deadline _____

Scholarship Application Deadline _____

Cost per 2 semesters (in-state or out-of-state Tuition, Fees, Books) _____

Cost per 2 semesters (Living Expenses) _____

Cost of equipment required (i.e. Laptop Computer) _____

Minimum GPA Requirement _____

Entrance Exams Required (i.e. SAT, ACT, GMAT, GRE, LSAT, MCAT) _____

Minimum Entrance Exam Score Required _____

Other Requirements for Admission _____
_____
_____
_____
_____
_____

Cost of Living Budget

The Cost of Living Budget can be used for *future planning* purposes, such as for determining whether you can afford your student loans, afford to purchase a car, or afford to purchase a home. The Cost of Living Budget can also be used for your *current situation*. Regardless, you will need to use realistic numbers, and if you do not use realistic numbers, you may be hurting your financial health, financial future, and perhaps employment prospects if you develop a bad credit record.

Instructions: The Cost of Living Budget should be completed very carefully. I recommend the below approach to the budget.

Step 1: Gross Income. Gross income is your pre-tax income. Complete the sections on gross income at the top of the budget and at the beginning of each "Obligations" category, except the Personal Lifetime Standard information which will be entered later.

Step 2: Taxes. Under "Housing" obligations, if you purchased a home, complete the line item on Property Taxes. If you rent the property, then the owner pays property taxes and you do not pay property taxes. Annual Property Taxes can be determined for a specific home by calling the county property tax office where the home is located. Taxes must be paid before anything else and that is why the tax line items are completed on the budget first.

Step 3: Taxes. Under "Other" obligations, complete the entire section on Taxes. Taxes must be paid before anything else and that is why the tax line items are completed on the budget first.

Step 4: Savings. Under "Other" obligations, complete the entire section on Savings. Completing the section on Savings will encourage you to set savings goals and achieve your savings goals.

Step 5: Expenses. Under "Other" obligations, complete the entire section on Expenses. This section may require you to *estimate* your expenses. You will need to use realistic numbers, and you can achieve this by talking with your parents, conducting internet searches of companies that offer the services you want, and in the case of purchasing a new home, you can contact utility companies about the specific home's billings for an entire year when the home was lived in. It is better to over-estimate your expenses (i.e. show a higher number than your bills might be) than to under-estimate your expenses, because you do *not* want your actual bills to be higher than what you estimated. If your actual bills are higher than what you estimated, then you may not have enough money to live.

Step 6: "Non-housing" Obligations. Complete the entire section on "Non-housing" obligations.

Step 7: "Housing" Obligations. Complete the entire section on "Housing" obligations. (In Step 2, you should have completed the property tax line item.)

Step 8: "Housing" Obligations Gross Income Limit. Under "Housing" obligations, are your TOTAL "Housing" obligations greater than FHA's limit of 31% of your gross income? The answer should be "no." -- As a teen, now is the time to set your own lifetime standards for how much you are willing to pay per month based on a percentage of your gross income. I personally recommend **"Housing" obligations be *no more than 20% of gross income*** when you have a lower income such as $40,000, but it is up to you to decide what you can afford. As your income rises, the percentage of gross income should be much less than 20%. I recommend by the time you turn 55, your home should be paid for and therefore, you should have no mortgage loans. (Keep in mind, even if you pay-off your mortgage, as long as you own the property, you will always have to pay property taxes.) Proceed to Step 9.

Step 9: Set and review your Personal Lifetime Standard for "Housing" obligations. Using the information in Step 8, complete these two sentences below and on the Cost of Living Budget. I hope you will select a percentage that is 20% of gross income or less, but it is up to you to decide.

"According to my Personal Lifetime Standard, my "Housing" obligations can be no more than _____% of my gross income. That means, I can spend no more than $_____ per month or $_____per year on "Housing" obligations."

Now, after reviewing your TOTAL "Housing" obligations on the budget, are your TOTAL "Housing" obligations greater than your Personal Lifetime Standard? The answer should be "no." If "Housing" obligations are greater than your Personal Lifetime Standard, then you will need to re-work the budget, using realistic numbers, until the TOTAL "Housing" obligations are no more than your Personal Lifetime Standard.

Step 10: "Non-housing" Obligations Gross Income Limit. Under "Non-housing" obligations, are your TOTAL "Non-housing" obligations greater than FHA's limit of 12% of gross income? The answer should be "no." -- With that said, I recommend **"Non-housing" obligations be no more than 11% of gross income** when you have a lower income such as $40,000, but it is up to you to decide what you can afford. As your income rises, the percentage of gross income used for "Non-housing" obligations should be much less than 11%. Be sure not to cheat yourself with credit cards. Credit cards can be convenient for paying expenses, but the cost of financing your purchases can be way too high. As a teen, now is the time to decide if you will pay-off your credit cards each month or if you will finance your purchases, throughout your lifetime. In addition, you will need to set your own lifetime standards for how much you are willing to pay per month for "Non-housing" obligations, based on a percentage of your gross income. Proceed to Step 11.

Step 11: Set and review your Personal Lifetime Standard for "Non-housing" obligations. Using the information in Step 10, complete these two sentences below and on the Cost of Living Budget. I hope you will select a percentage that is 11% of gross income or less, but it is up to you to decide.

"According to my Personal Lifetime Standard, my "Non-housing" obligations can be no more than _____% of my gross income. That means, I can spend no more than $_____ per month or $_____ per year on "Non-housing" obligations."

Now, after reviewing your TOTAL "Non-housing" obligations, are your TOTAL "Non-housing" obligations greater than your Personal Lifetime Standard? The answer should be "no." If "Non-housing" obligations are greater than your Personal Lifetime Standard, then you will need to re-work the budget, using realistic numbers, until the TOTAL "Non-housing" obligations are no more than your Personal Lifetime Standard.

Step 12: Complete all of Steps 1 – 11 again and repeat Steps 1 - 11, until you are satisfied all of your numbers are realistic.

IMPORTANT NOTES:
You will need to include all expected expenses in the budget. If there is not a line item in the budget for the expected expense, you will need to create a line item in the budget.

Once you are married, you may want to consider taking out loans based on one person's BASE salary. (BASE salary does not include any bonuses provided for good work performance.) That way, if one spouse loses a job, then you will still be able to pay your obligations.

Remember, what you save and spend is up to you. Never let any entity or person tell you that you can afford more, if you cannot. By completing this budget, you will be able to better understand what you can afford. Companies and people tend to take advantage of the young, because they are less experienced, and the elderly, because they are perceived, although incorrectly, to be weak and too trusting. Learning how to budget is your chance to be a step ahead and to feel more secure.

Cost of Living Budget

Please read the instructions on pages 159 and 160 before completing this form.

This budget is based on the Federal Housing Administration's (FHA's) housing formula and should be used as a guideline only. "Housing" and "Non-housing" long term obligations should *not* total more than 43% of your total gross income, based on FHA's formula. I would recommend you spend much less than 43% of your total gross income on "Housing" and "Non-housing" to keep your debt low, maintain a good credit score, and keep your options open.

My gross income is _____ per year.

My gross income is _____ per month.

(Gross income is also known as pre-tax income.)

"Housing" Obligations

"Housing" obligations should be **no more than 31% of gross income**, based on FHA's formula. 31% of my gross income is equal to _____. My "Housing" obligations can be no more than $_____ per month or $_____ per year.

Personal Lifetime Standard. According to my Personal Lifetime Standard, my "Housing" obligations can be no more than _____% of my gross income. That means, I can spend no more than $_____ per month or $_____ per year on "Housing" obligations.

	Monthly	Annually
Apartment Rent or Mortgage loan payment if you purchased a home		
Homeowner's Association fees or Condo fees (Generally, this is for maintenance and upkeep of the grounds and building)		
Renter's Insurance if you rent or Homeowner's Insurance if you purchased a home		
Flood Insurance or other required insurance		
Mortgage Insurance if you purchased a home and you put less than 20% down on the purchase price of the home		
Property taxes, if you purchased the property (If you rent a property, the owner pays property taxes.)		
Any land lease fees (Sometimes a home purchased sits on property that belongs to someone else, and consequently, the homeowner must pay land lease fees. This is not very common but you should make sure any home you purchase does not require you to lease the land.)		
TOTAL		

"Non-housing" Obligations

"Non-housing" obligations should be **no more than 12% of gross income**, based on FHA's formula. 12% of my gross income is equal to _____. My "Non-housing" obligations can be no more than $_____ per month or $_____ per year.

Personal Lifetime Standard. According to my Personal Lifetime Standard, my "Housing" obligations can be no more than _____% of my gross income. That means, I can spend no more than $_____ per month or $_____ per year on "Housing" obligations.

	Monthly	Annually
Student Loan Payment		
Credit Card Loan Payment (If you do not pay off your credit card each month, this is considered a loan. Borrowing from your credit card can make it difficult to pay-off, because interest rates are often around 20% per year.)		
Car Loan Payment		
Alimony		
Child Support		
Other loans and long term obligations		
TOTAL		

"Other" Obligations

The "Other" obligations include obligations to yourself, such as for savings, and to others. **If you spend exactly 31% of gross income on "Housing" and exactly 12% of gross income on "Non-housing" then you would spend 57% of your gross income on "Other" obligations.** The total percentages of these three categories must add up to 100%, otherwise you will get yourself into trouble. (100% - 31% - 12% = 57%).

____% of my gross income is equal to _____.

My "other" obligations can be no more than _____ per month or _____ per year.

TAXES (Taxes are deducted from your paycheck automatically. You will need to verify the taxes are withheld in the correct amounts each month. You will need to consider taxes when budgeting.)	Monthly	Annually
Federal Income Taxes (Internal Revenue Service)		
State Income Taxes (This is the state in which you live and work. State income taxes can be zero or high, such as 5.5%.)		
Local Income Taxes (This is the township or city in which you live and work. Not all localities have income taxes.)		
Social Security and Medicare Taxes (This is currently a flat rate of 7.65% of income received from an employer.)		
Medicaid (This is specific to the state in which you live and work. Not all states have Medicaid and not all states tax for Medicaid through income.)		

BERNTZEN

Cost of Living Budget

SAVINGS - Short Term and Long Term	Monthly	Annually
Short Term		
One (1) Year of "housing," "non-housing," and "other" (taxes you owe, and required living expenses) obligations from your expected budget should be saved throughout your lifetime. You should have this as cash on hand. -- I need to save a total of $_____. I plan to save the total amount within _____ months.		
Down payment for a car. -- I need to save a total of $_____. I plan to save the total amount within _____ months.		
Down payment for a home (10% or 20% of the purchase price). -- I need to save a total of $_____. I plan to save the total amount within _____ months.		
Nice furniture to last a lifetime. -- I need to save a total of $_____. I plan to save the total amount within _____ months.		
Home maintenance, such as painting and a new roof. -- I need to save a total of $_____. I plan to save the total amount within _____ months.		
Home electronics. -- I need to save a total of $_____. I plan to save the total amount within _____ months.		
Vacation. -- I need to save a total of $_____. I plan to save the total amount within _____ months.		
Other needs. -- I need to save a total of $_____. I plan to save the total amount within _____ months.		
Other needs. -- I need to save a total of $_____. I plan to save the total amount within _____ months.		
Long Term - Retirement		
IRA (Individual Retirement Account). You set-up an IRA account through a brokerage firm and can contribute up to a certain amount per year as required by law.		
401k. You and your employer contribute to a 401k retirement account that is set-up for you with a brokerage firm. Your employer may match a certain percentage of what you contribute. (Include only your contributions here. Do not include your employer's contributions here.)		
Stock or Mutual Fund Account through a brokerage firm		
Cash held in an interest bearing account		

EXPENSES	Monthly	Annually
Car Insurance		
Health Insurance		
Medical expenses including prescriptions not covered by health insurance		
Food / Groceries		
Fuel for Car		
Entertainment and Dining Out		
Cable		
High Speed Internet Access		
Land line phone		
Cell phone		
Water service		
Trash service		
Gas service		
Electricity		
Clothes		
Shoes		
Laundry and Dry cleaning		
Other needs and obligations		
Other needs and obligations		
Other needs and obligations		
Other needs and obligations		
TOTAL (Taxes, Savings, Expenses)		

	Monthly	Annually
TOTAL OBLIGATIONS ("Housing", "Non-housing", and "Other" Obligations)		
GROSS INCOME (from the top of the worksheet)		

For Budgeting purposes, Total Obligations should equal Gross Income. (You must always consider the cost of taking loans including fees, penalties such as paying off a loan early, and interest rates. High interest rates, starting at 10% can keep you in the hole longer and interest rates at 15% or higher can bankrupt you, depending on how much you make and how much you borrowed.) Any interest you pay to a credit card company is less money you could have saved for short term or long term purchases.

Example - College, Career, and Money Plan Worksheet

NOTE: The completed example on this page and the following pages is based on the sample resumes in this book, because I would like for you to see how the College, Career, and Money Plan contributes to the resume. It is important to note it is uncommon that any one person gets the exact job and responsibilities they planned for. It can happen, but usually there is a variation in job titles and responsibilities, as companies are different from the other and companies are constantly evolving. -- Just as companies are constantly evolving, WE, as individuals, are constantly evolving and therefore we can change and should change our plan to best suit our needs and interests in high school, college, and throughout our professional careers. It would be unusual for any one person to NOT change their plan at some point in their lives. However, with that said, it is important to have a written plan and work toward your plan's goals. By having a written plan, you are more likely to be successful in achieving your goals or nearing your goals, than if you did not have a plan at all.

Refer to Page #

9

What are your interests?
Volunteer work, fundraising, goal-setting/earning badges, speaking Spanish, leading a group of people, speaking in front of people, organizing, writing

10

What field or industry do you want to work in?
not-for-profit community organization

What are your values?

11

I enjoy working with all people in all types of settings. I want my employer to be good to its employees, and in good standing with the community. I need an employer who has a good tuition reimbursement program for when I seek my MBA. I need an employer who offers a good health insurance plan and retirement plan (401k plan).

12

Do you have any limitations?
NO!

What is your deal and ultimate job?

12, 18

Vice President of Development Services

12, 13

What specifically do you want to do in your ideal and ultimate job and why?
I want to raise money for the not-for-profit organization I work for. I want to lead a team of people to accomplish the organization's goals.

18

What degree(s) are required to get your ideal and ultimate job? What will be your major or area of concentration?
I will need a Bachelor's degree in business. Specifically, I want a BS with a major in Management. Eventually, I will need an MBA to be promoted to executive management.

4

How many years will it take to get each degree? Will you complete all degrees consecutively or will you work for a number of years between each degree? What is your plan?
It will take 4 years to get my BS in Management. It will take one to four years to get my MBA, depending on if I go part-time or full-time or if I get admitted to the Executive MBA program. I will plan to work for about 4 or 5 years before I seek my MBA. When I get my MBA depends on which employer I am with, if the employer is supportive, and if my employer will pay for all or part of my MBA.

Example - College, Career, and Money Plan Worksheet

CAREER PATH – What is the expected career path to achieve your ideal and ultimate job?

Refer to Page #	Stage in Life	Expected Job Title	Job Responsibilities	# of Years or Range of Years Expected in Job	$ Expected Annual Salary / Salary Range	Type of Degree and Major Required to Get the Job	Experience and Job Skills Required to Get the Job	Licensures, Registrations, Certifications Required / Recommended to Get the Job, if Any
13 - 20, 101 - 103	**During High School**							
118	H.S. job (related to ideal and ultimate job)	Intern	To perform administrative tasks related to fundraising	One Summer	$10 per hour	None	Must be organized and able to type. Familiar with MS Excel, Access, Word. Analytical skills. Quality-oriented.	None
	H.S. job (related to ideal and ultimate job)	Intern	To perform administrative tasks related to fundraising	One Summer	None	Working toward college degree	Analytical skills, writing skills, and presentation skills. Quality-oriented.	None
	During College							
	College job (related to ideal and ultimate job)	Intern	To perform administrative tasks related to fundraising	One Summer	$12 per hour	Working toward college degree	Analytical skills, writing skills, people skills, presentation skills. Quality-oriented.	None
	College job (related to ideal and ultimate job)	Intern	To perform administrative tasks related to fundraising	One Summer	$13 per hour	Working toward college degree	Analytical skills, writing skills, people skills, presentation skills. Quality-oriented.	None
	Degreed Professional							
	1st job (related to ideal and ultimate job)	Analyst, Fundraising Development	To write grant proposals and secure grant funding	2 – 4 Years	$40,000 - $50,000 per year	BS Business or BA Economics or similar	Analytical skills, meeting facilitation skills, writing skills, people skills, organization skills, presentation skills. Quality-oriented.	None
	2nd job (related to ideal and ultimate job)	Manager, Fundraising Development	To write grant proposals and secure grant funding. Perform analytical work at a higher level.	2 – 5 Years	$50,000 - $70,000 per year	BS Business or BA Economics or similar	Analytical skills, meeting facilitation skills, writing skills, people skills, organization skills, presentation skills. Quality-oriented.	None
	3rd job (related to ideal and ultimate job)	Director, Fundraising Development	To lead grant-writing teams, responsible for raising more than $20 million per year.	4 – 8 Years	$70,000 - $85,000 per year	BS or BA and MBA	Analytical skills, meeting facilitation skills, writing skills, people skills, organization skills, presentation skills. Quality-oriented.	None
	4th job (related to ideal and ultimate job)	-						
	5th job (related to ideal and ultimate job)	-						
	6th job (related to ideal and ultimate job)	-						
	Ideal and ultimate job	Vice President, Fundraising	To lead the strategic planning process. To lead the organization in raising more than $70 million per year.	5 – 10 Years	$85,000 - $120,000 per year	BS or BA and MBA	Analytical skills, meeting facilitation skills, writing skills, people skills, organization skills, presentation skills. Quality-oriented.	None

Example - College, Career, and Money Plan Worksheet

COLLEGE CONSIDERATION

The colleges I am considering for my bachelor's degree include:

University of Illinois at Chicago	Purdue University	Iowa
Northwestern University	UCLA	Michigan State
University of Chicago	Columbia University	University of NC
DePaul University	Duke University	Arizona State University
University of Texas at Austin	Cornell	University of Washington Seattle

The colleges I am considering for my master's degree include:

University of Illinois at Chicago	Purdue University	Iowa
Northwestern University	UCLA	Michigan State
University of Chicago	Columbia University	University of NC
DePaul University	Duke University	Arizona State University
University of Texas at Austin	Cornell	University of Washington Seattle

The colleges I am considering for my PhD or other doctoral degree include:

Does not apply to me.

Some colleges are very competitive and therefore you need to apply to many colleges to ensure you will be accepted.

BERNTZEN

Example - College, Career, and Money Plan Worksheet

COLLEGE ADMISSION REQUIREMENTS

Instructions: For each degree and college you are considering, please complete this information. The information can be obtained from the college's website.

Name of College
University of Texas at Austin

Degree
BS (Bachelor of Science)

Major or Concentration
Management

Application Deadline
Application due December 1, 2011 in order to be admitted in the Fall 2012

Scholarship Application Deadline
Application due December 1, 2011 for Fall 2012 Admission

Cost per 2 semesters (in-state or out-of-state Tuition, Fees, Books)
In-state tuition and fees (Resident) $9,000; Books $1,000

Cost per 2 semesters (Living Expenses)
$12,000

Cost of equipment required (i.e. Laptop Computer)
$1,000 Laptop Computer

Minimum GPA Requirement
None. Must be in top 10% of Texas high school class to be admitted to university but not to major.

Entrance Exams Required (i.e. SAT, ACT, GMAT, GRE, LSAT, MCAT)
SAT Reasoning Test or ACT (including writing test). Official scores must be received by the University Application for Admission Deadline.

Minimum Entrance Exam Score Required
No minimum test score. Must get a high test score to be competitive.

Other Requirements for Admission
I must take these required courses in high school: http://bealonghorn.utexas.edu/freshmen/admission/hs-courses/
I must take math and science courses each year in high school.
Must be ranked in the top 10% of a Texas high school class to be admitted to the university, not to a business major.
Must be ranked higher than 10% to be admitted as a business major as it is highly competitive with
few spaces available. The highest ranked have the best chance of being accepted as a business major,
combined with high test scores, leadership activities, honors, awards, community service, work history
2 Essays
Official high school transcript

SAT Reasoning Test
ACT (including writing test)
$60 application fee (fee can be waived for financial need)
Resume detailing extracurricular activities, leadership activities, honors, awards, community service, work history
Letters of Recommendation (References)
Extracurricular activities, community service and other leadership activities, work history, honors, awards

Example – College, Career, and Money Plan Worksheet

Refer to Page #	
	CAN I AFFORD MY STUDENT LOANS?
19, 102	What is your Expected *Annual* Salary for your 1st job as a Degreed Professional?
	$40,000 - $50,000 in Chicago. (This salary may be lower in other parts of the country.) I want to live in Chicago where I have the option to work with many larger not-for-profit organizations.
	What is your Expected *Monthly* Salary for your 1st job as a Degreed Professional? Hint: Take the Annual Salary and divide by 12 months. I will use $40,000 as my annual salary because I want to be safe. $40,000 / 12 months = $3,333 is my monthly salary.
	Will you take out any student loans? If yes, what is the total amount you expect to borrow in student loans?
	Yes. I will take out a total of $20,000 in student loans for my bachelor's degree. Since I will be working between getting my BS and MBA, I do not expect to borrow money for my MBA. I will save some money to pay for part of my MBA. It will be important to select an employer who has a good tuition reimbursement program that meets my needs.
69, 73	From the Table on **Calculating Loan Payments**, what will be your *monthly* student loan payment after you graduate from college?
	I will borrow $20,000. I will pay back the loan in 10 years. I expect a fixed interest rate no more than 6.5%. Based on this information, my monthly student loan payment will be $227.10. (SEE PAGE 168.)
159 - 162	Using the **Cost of Living Budget**, will you be able to make your *monthly* student loan payments based on the *monthly* salary from your 1st job as a Degreed Professional? In other words, will you have enough money to pay your student loan, pay taxes, pay rent, buy food, etc.?*
	Yes, I will be able to make my monthly student loan payment and will be able to support myself. I calculated my Cost of Living Budget (SEE PAGE 169), inserting my monthly student loan payment and the lowest expected salary I expect to receive from my 1st job as a Degreed Professional. After running the numbers in the Cost of Living Budget, I feel like I can save money for my financial goals and work toward my career goals. I will have to go to a good but inexpensive college so that I do not exceed the $20,000 I am borrowing. When it is time to seriously shop for student loans, I will diligently look for the absolute lowest fixed interest rate. I will be working while I am in college when I can, but I will not make very much money. However, I can apply for scholarships as I know every little bit helps, but I cannot count on scholarships.

*If you will *not* be able to make your monthly student loan payments based on the Cost of Living Budget, then consider going to a less expensive college that can still help you get the career you want or consider a combination of scholarships and working. As a last resort consider changing careers to one that pays more in salary, if you cannot figure out how to get the finances to work.

168

Example – Loan Calculation

(Hint: Use the easy Excel formulas presented in the table on Calculating Loan Payments on page 73 - 78.)

Loan Amount	$20,000.00 Dollars
Loan Term	10.00 Years
Interest Rate	6.50% %
Monthly Payment:	$227.10
Total Payments (interest and principal)	$27,251.51
Total Interest Paid	$7,251.51

Example – Cost of Living Budget

Please read the instructions on pages 159 and 160 before completing this form.

This budget is based on the Federal Housing Administration's (FHA's) housing formula and should be used as a guideline only.

"Housing" and "Non-housing" long term obligations should *not* total more than 43% of your total gross income, based on FHA's formula.

I would recommend you spend much less than 43% of your total gross income on "Housing" and "Non-housing" to keep your debt low, maintain a good credit score, and keep your options open.

My gross income is _____$40,000_____ per year.

My gross income is _____$3,333_____ per month.

(Gross income is also known as pre-tax income.)

"Housing" Obligations

"Housing" obligations should be **no more than 31% of gross income,** based on FHA's formula.

31% of my gross income is equal to $12,400 per year . .31 x $40,000 per year = $12,400 per year

My "Housing" obligations can be no more than $ 1,033.23 per month or $ 12,400 per year. $12,400 / 12 months = $1033.23 per month

Personal Lifetime Standard. According to my Personal Lifetime Standard, my "Housing" obligations can be no more than 20 % of my gross income. That means, I can spend no more than $ 666 per month or $ 8,000 per year on "Housing" obligations. .20 x $40,000 per year = $8,000 per year. $8,000 / 12 months = $666 per month

	Monthly	Annually	
Apartment Rent or Mortgage loan payment if you purchased a home	$ 500.00	6,000.00	I estimated rent based on the apartments for rent I read about in the local newspaper classified section. I could rent a 2 bedroom / 2 bath apartment for $1000 per month in a high cost area. I will choose to have a roommate my first couple years after college in order to save money. Therefore I estimate my rent will be $500 per month. $500 per month x 12 months = $6,000 per year
Homeowner's Association fees or Condo fees (Generally, this is for maintenance and upkeep of the grounds and building)	$ -	0.00	
Renter's Insurance if you rent or Homeowner's Insurance if you purchased a home	$ 50.00	600.00	I called my family's insurance agent and asked how much renter's insurance was. The cost $50 per month x 12 months = $600 per year.
Flood Insurance or other required insurance	$ -	0.00	
Mortgage Insurance if you purchased a home and you put less than 20% down on the purchase price of the home	$ -	0.00	
Property taxes, if you purchased the property (If you rent a property, the owner pays property taxes.)	$ -	0.00	
Any land lease fees (Sometimes a home purchased sits on property that belongs to someone else, and consequently, the homeowner must pay land lease fees. This is not very common but you should make sure any home you purchase does not require you to lease	$ -	0.00	
TOTAL	$ 550.00	6,600.00	

My "Housing" obligations are **16.5% of gross income.**

$6,600 / $40,000 = .165 Expressed as a percentage = 16.5%

I fall under my Personal Lifetime Standard of 20% of my gross income. This is good, because I will need money for my "Other" obligations.

Example – Cost of Living Budget

"Non-housing" Obligations

Non-housing obligations should be **no more than 12% of gross income**, based on FHA's formula.

12% of my gross income is equal to $4,800 per year.

.12 x $40,000 per year = $4,800 per year

My "non-housing" obligations can be no more than $400 per month or $4,800 per year.

$4,800 / 12 months = $400 per month

Personal Lifetime Standard. According to my Personal Lifetime Standard, my "Housing" obligations can be no more than ___11___ % of my gross income. That means, I can spend no more than $ __4,400__ per month or $ __366.66__ per year on "Housing" obligations.

.11 x $40,000 per year = $4,400 per year. $4,400 / 12 months = $366.66

	Monthly	Annually	
Student Loan Payment	$ 227.10	2,725.20	Calculate loan payments in Excel using the formulas provided from the table on Calculating Loan Payments.
Credit Card Loan Payment (If you do not pay off your credit card each month, this is considered a loan. Borrowing from your credit card can make it difficult to pay-off, because interest rates are often around 20% per year.)	$ -	0.00	
Car Loan Payment	$ -	0.00	I plan to drive the new car my parents gave me in high school for 10 years.
Alimony	$ -	0.00	
Child Support	$ -	0.00	
Other loans and long term obligations	$ -	0.00	
TOTAL	$ 227.10	2,725.20	

My "Non-housing" obligations are 6.813% of gross income.

$2,725.20 / $40,000 = .06813 Expressed as a percentage = 6.813%

I fall under my Personal Lifetime Standard of 11% of my gross income. This is good, because I will need money for my "Other" obligations.

Example – Cost of Living Budget

"Other" Obligations

The "Other" obligations include obligations to yourself, such as for savings, and to others. **If you spend exactly 31% of gross income on "housing" and exactly 12% of gross income on "non-housing" then you would spend 57% of your gross income on "other" obligations.** The total percentages of these three categories must add up to 100%, otherwise you will get yourself into trouble. (100% - 31% - 12% = 57%).

57% of my gross income is equal to _____.

My "other" obligations can be no more than _____ per month or _____ per year.

I plan to spend ___16.5%___ of gross income on "housing" and __6.813%__ of gross income on "non-housing." The total percentage of my gross income I will spend on "housing" and "non-housing" is 16.5% + 6.813% = 23.313%.

For budgeting purposes, I must allocate (distribute) every dollar I make in gross income. Therefore, 100% of gross income - 23.313% of gross income = 76.687% of gross income. The rest of my gross income, 76.687%, will go to "other" obligations.

76.687% of my gross income is equal to $30,674.80 per year.

My "other" obligations can be no more than __$2,556.23__ per month or _$30,674.80_ per year.

I will ignore this because I am spending a lot less than 31% of gross income on "housing" and a lot less than 12% of gross income on "non-housing" simply because I cannot afford it. I have "other" obligations that are required for me to live.

.76687x $40,000 = $30,674.80

$30,674.80 / 12 months = $2,556.23

TAXES (Taxes are deducted from your paycheck automatically. You will need to verify the taxes are withheld in the correct amounts each month. You will need to consider taxes when budgeting.)	Monthly		Annually		
Federal Income Taxes (Internal Revenue Service)	$	362.08	$	4,345.00	I estimated a 10.8625% effective tax rate by reading the instructions and completing the 1040EZ form on the IRS website.
State Income Taxes (This is the state in which you live and work. State income taxes can be zero or high, such as 5.5%.)	$	100.00	$	1,200.00	The state where I expect to work has a flat tax rate at 3%. I went to the state's Department of Revenue website and completed the 1040 form to learn this. $40,000 per year x .03 state tax rate = $1,200 per year
Local Income Taxes (This is the township or city in which you ive and work. Not all localities have income taxes.)	$	-	$	-	
Social Security and Medicare Taxes (This is currently a flat rate of 7.65% of income received from an employer.)	$	255.00	$	3,060.00	$40,000 x .0765 = $3,060
Medicaid (This is specific to the state in which you live and work. Not all states have Medicaid and not all states tax for Medicaid through income.)	$	-	$	-	

BERNTZEN

Example – Cost of Living Budget

SAVINGS - Short Term and Long Term	Monthly	Annually
Short Term		
One (1) Year of "housing," "non-housing," and "other" (taxes you owe, and required living expenses) obligations from your expected budget should be saved throughout your lifetime. You should have this as cash on hand. -- I need to save a total of $26,395____. I plan to save the total amount within ___64__ months. (I expect my employer to withhold taxes at the correct amount each month, and I will verify this. Therefore, I do not need to save the tax portion.)	$416.66	$5,000.00
Down payment for a car. -- I need to save a total of $_____, I plan to save the total amount within _____ months.		
Down payment for a home (10% or 20% of the purchase price). -- I need to save a total of $_____. I plan to save the total amount within _____ months.		
Nice furniture to last a lifetime. -- I need to save a total of $_____. I plan to save the total amount within _____ months.		
Home maintenance, such as painting and a new roof. -- I need to save a total of $_____. I plan to save the total amount within _____ months.		
Home electronics. -- I need to save a total of $_____, I plan to save the total amount within _____ months.		
Vacation. -- I need to save a total of $_____, I plan to save the total amount within _____ months.		
Other needs. -- I need to save a total of $_____, I plan to save the total amount within _____ months.		
Other needs. -- I need to save a total of $_____, I plan to save the total amount within _____ months.		
Long Term - Retirement		
IRA (Individual Retirement Account). You set-up an IRA account through a brokerage firm and can contribute up to a certain amount per year as required by law.		
401k. You and your employer contribute to a 401k retirement account that is set-up for you with a brokerage firm. Your employer may match a certain percentage of what you contribute. (Include only your contributions here. Do not include your employer's contributions here.)	$ 100.00	$1,200
Stock or Mutual Fund Account through a brokerage firm		
Cash held in an interest bearing account		

$40,000 salary - $5,000 savings - $8,605.00 taxes withheld from my paycheck = $26,395 to be saved as cash in an interest bearing account in case I lose my job, as I will need to continue to pay my obligations.

I will plan to contribute 3% of my salary per year. That is, .03 x $40,000 = $1,200

Example – Cost of Living Budget

EXPENSES	Monthly		Annually	
Car Insurance	$	100.00	$	1,200.00
Health Insurance	$	100.00	$	1,200.00
Medical expenses including prescriptions not covered by health insurance	$	25.00	$	300.00
Food / Groceries	$	400.00	$	4,800.00
Fuel for Car	$	170.00	$	2,040.00
Entertainment and Dining Out	$	197.00	$	2,364.00
Cable			$	-
High Speed Internet Access			$	-
Land line phone			$	-
Cell phone	$	60.00	$	720.00
Water service	$	25.00	$	300.00
Trash service	$	7.00	$	84.00
Gas service	$	80.00	$	960.00
Electricity	$	80.00	$	960.00
Clothes			$	-
Shoes			$	-
Laundry and Dry cleaning	$	78.00	$	936.00
Other needs and obligations			$	-
Other needs and obligations			$	-
Other needs and obligations			$	-
Other needs and obligations			$	-
TOTAL (Taxes, Savings, Expenses)	$	2,555.74	$	30,669.00

My parents said they would buy me some good quality career clothes and a few casual pieces as a college graduation present. I do not expect to buy new clothes for about one year.

TOTAL OBLIGATIONS ("Housing", "Non-housing", and "Other" Obligations)	$	3,332.84	$	40,000.00	Rounded up
GROSS INCOME (from the top of the worksheet)	$	3,333.00	$	40,000.00	Rounded up

For Budgeting purposes, Total Obligations should equal Gross Income. (You must always consider the cost of taking loans including fees, penalties such as paying off a loan early, and interest rates. High interest rates, starting at 10% can keep you in the hole longer and interest rates at 15% or higher can bankrupt you, depending on how much you make and how much you borrowed.) Any interest you pay to a credit card company is less money you could have saved for short term or long term purchases.

Example - College, Career, and Money Plan Worksheet

STATE YOUR GOALS TO ACHIEVE

<u>GPA and Test Scores</u>

Refer to Page #

80

My target GPA for high school is a __3.8__ out of _4.0_. I do not want my GPA to be less than 3.6.

Hint: Make your target GPA higher than the minimum GPA requirement or target for the colleges of your choice.

The Entrance Exam(s) required for undergraduate (bachelor's degree) admissions include(s):

SAT
_____

My target Entrance Exam / Test Score is

1300. Even though some of the colleges I am applying to do not have a minimum, I know I need to score high in order to be accepted.

Hint: Make your target score higher than the minimum score or target required for the colleges of your choice.

My target GPA for my bachelor's degree is a __4.0__ out of _4.0_. I do not want my GPA to be less than 3.5.

Hint: Bachelor's degree GPA's should be no less than a 3.0 out of 4.0 in order to be a desirable job candidate.

A GPA of 3.25 or higher out of 4.0 is preferred in order to be a more desirable job candidate.

The Entrance Exam(s) required for graduate degree (master's, PhD, or other doctoral degree) admissions include(s):

GMAT
_____

My target Entrance Exam / Test Score is

I will research and complete this about one year before I plan to begin graduate school.

Hint: Make your target score higher than the minimum score required for the colleges of your choice.

My target GPA for my graduate degree is a _____ out of _____.

Hint: Graduate degree GPA's should be no less than a 3.5 out of 4.0.

Example - College, Career, and Money Plan Worksheet

STATE YOUR GOALS TO ACHIEVE

<u>Leadership</u>

Enter the type of Leadership experience you would like to pursue in high school, college, and as a degreed professional. Once you have the leadership experience, you can advertise it on your resume to help you get the job and the career you want.   Leadership should display initiative and follow-through. (You started at your own suggestion and finished something with success.) When will you pursue and accomplish your leadership experience?

Refer to Page #		During High School		Year
84		High School leadership	Girl Scouts - I will suggest and organize a Holiday Dinner for the elderly by 2009.	2009
		High School leadership	Girl Scouts - I will seek to sell the most cookies in the state of Texas in 2007 & 2008.	2007 & 2008
		High School leadership	I will seek to become the President of the Spanish Club to get experience leading club meetings in 2009, and I will suggest and organize the first-ever fund-raiser.	2009
		High School leadership	I will target to work with Habitat for Humanity in the Summer 2011 to build a house in a Spanish speaking country to use my language skills.	2011

Example - College, Career, and Money Plan Worksheet

During College

College leadership	I will plan to become the President of a campus organization as a Freshman. I have to get on campus early and check-out the organizations.	Freshman
College leadership	I will plan to work with a not-for-profit organization for my Winter Break as a Freshman to work in a Spanish speaking country to use my language skills. I would like to build another house or do something with my hands.	Freshman - Winter Break
College leadership	I will plan to lead a team of people to organize a campus event. I will have to find a campus organization to do this at the beginning of my Sophomore year.	Sophomore
College leadership	In all jobs I undertake, I will make a point to volunteer to lead a group or organize an event or take on additional work to build my skills.	All Jobs - All Years

Degreed Professional

Extracurricular Activity leadership	I will set goals for myself at least once each year after I receive my degree. Right now, I have no idea.	_____
Extracurricular Activity leadership	_____	_____
Extracurricular Activity leadership	_____	_____
Extracurricular Activity leadership	_____	_____
Extracurricular Activity leadership	_____	_____
Extracurricular Activity leadership	_____	_____

Example - College, Career, and Money Plan Worksheet

STATE YOUR GOALS TO ACHIEVE

Behaviors

Enter two (2) behaviors you want to improve on each year. How will you do it? When will you do it? Go back at the end of each year to see if you accomplished your goal. You can do this throughout your lifetime.

Refer to Page #
120, 123

Behavior	How	Year
I want to overcome my fear of talking in front of others.	1. I will run for President of the Spanish Club so that I can lead meetings. 2. I will take a Speech course.	2009
I want to become more responsible.	I will focus on doing exactly what I said I would do, by when I said I would do it. Deep down I know I can do this.	2009

178

Definitions

AP (Advanced Placement) – You can take AP courses in high school and then take the AP exam. Your score on the AP exam will determine if a college will give you college credit for the course. Ask the colleges you are considering if they accept AP courses for credit and what your score needs to be. Colleges will limit the number of credit hours you can receive for AP. Go to www.collegeboard.com for more information.

APR (Annual Percentage Rate) - The APR is another way of looking at *interest charged to you for loans*, whether the rate is fixed or adjustable (variable, changing). The APR is a calculation you can find on FDIC's website, www.fdic.gov, in the document *Determination of Annual Percentage Rate*. FDIC regulates how financial institutions can calculate the APR. The APR is annualized (expressed as a yearly rate), and takes into account the interest rate as well as charges and *some* fees. Loan contracts, such as a mortgage contract, list the interest rate, not the APR.

APY (Annual Percentage Yield) – The APY is another way of looking at *interest earned by you in an interest bearing bank account*, whether the rate is fixed or adjustable (variable, changing). The APY is a calculation you can find on FDIC's website, www.fdic.gov, in the document *Annual Percentage Yield Calculation*. FDIC regulates how financial institutions can calculate the APY. The APY is a bank's calculation based on the current advertised interest rate and considers planned changes, such as tiered and stepped interest rates.

Annualized – Annualized is a term used to express a yearly rate.

Annualized Gain or Loss – If you calculate the percentage gain or loss on an investment in terms of how much you earned or lost each year, this is your gain or loss. For example, if you invested in real estate, purchased it for $50,000, and then sold it five years later for $75,000, your overall investment gain was $25,000. Your annualized gain was $5000 ($25,000 / 5 years = $5000). To calculate your *overall* gain as a *percent*, which is what you most likely are interested in for planning purposes, you take your overall investment gain of $25,000 and divide it by your initial investment of $50,000. Your overall gain was 50%. To determine what percent you gained each year, the *annualized gain*, divide 50% / 5 years, which equals 10%. You had a 10% annualized gain. You do these calculations to understand and measure the success of your investments. You can also subtract any taxes, such as capital gains taxes and property taxes, when determining your overall annualized investment gain.

Associate's Degree – An associate's degree is a two year degree, usually obtained from a community college. The associate's degree can be pursued after high school.

Bachelor's Degree – A bachelor's degree is a four year degree, obtained from a college or university. Some community colleges offer four year degrees. A bachelor's degree can be pursued after high school.

Budget - A budget is a specific amount of money that you have *planned* to spend on a certain item, group of items, or service(s) for a period of time. Examples of budgets include a housing budget, expense budget, maintenance budget, grocery budget, entertainment budget, vacation budget. These examples make up an overall household budget or Cost of Living Budget. At the end of your budgeting period, it is a good idea to compare what you *actually spent* with what you *planned* to spend in your budget. If all goes well, you will have spent less than you planned for in the budget.

CLEP (College Level Examination Program) – Some colleges allow you to place out of courses by taking CLEP exams. Currently, there are 33 different exams you can take, from American Literature and History, to Economics and Psychology. Go to www.collegeboard.com for more information. Colleges have a limit on the number of hours they will award you based on CLEP exams.

Calculating Loan Payments – You should calculate what your expected monthly loan payments would be, before taking out a student loan or any loan, such as a car loan or mortgage. The calculation in Table 11 is for *fixed and adjustable* interest rate loans. A fixed interest rate means the interest rate is always the *same* throughout the life of the loan. An adjustable or variable interest rate is tied to a key financial indicator in the marketplace, such as the prime rate, of which you have no control. Adjustable or variable interest rate loans are not recommended, because these loans have *changing* interest rates, and you do not know the future interest rate. However, most likely the interest rate will go up.

Career – A career is a series of jobs in the same field or industry.

Career Path - The sequence of jobs leading up to your ideal and ultimate job is the career path.

Collateral – If a borrower fails to make loan payments, the collateral or the asset with which a loan was secured, can be seized by the lender. Collateral is the asset you, as a borrower, offer to the lender to secure your loan. There are secured and unsecured loans. Unsecured loans do not require you to have collateral.

Definitions (Cont'd)

College, Career, and Money Plan Worksheet – The College, Career, and Money Plan Worksheet is a tool that can be used for college planning, career planning, financial planning, and money management.

Cost of Living Budget – The Cost of Living Budget is used to *plan* for a future situation, such as obtaining student loans, purchasing a car or purchasing a home for a period of time, usually one year. The Cost of Living Budget is also used to *plan* for a current situation, for a period of time, usually one year. You should go back at the end of the year and compare what you actually spent with what you planned to spend. If all goes well, you will have spent less than you planned to spend in the budget.

Culture, Work – A work culture is how and how well employees work together, and how the company treats its employees and customers.

Degree – A degree is a reward one receives for hard work. The degree can be from high school or college.

Degreed Professional – A degreed professional is someone who has completed a college degree and is working full-time.

Disposable Income – Disposable income is your income after paying taxes. The taxes included in this calculation are federal income taxes, state income taxes, FICA, property taxes, and other personal taxes such as license taxes.[9,10] There are two things you can do with your disposable income, income after paying taxes, and that is to save it or spend it.

Earnings or Earning – Earnings or Earning can be used interchangeably with income in this book.

Effective Tax Rate – Calculating the effective tax rate is just a way of understanding how much you pay in taxes with respect to your gross income. The effective tax rate is not an IRS calculation, but it is a calculation to be used for your own planning and budgeting purposes. You can calculate an effective tax rate for any one tax paid divided by your gross income. You can also calculate an effective tax rate for any group of taxes paid divided by your gross income. For example, the *federal* effective income tax rate is the total amount paid in federal income taxes divided by your gross income. As another example, your total effective *income* tax rate is the total amount paid in federal, state, and local income taxes divided by your gross income. You can also calculate a total effective tax rate for all taxes paid or to be paid. If you know the total dollar amount of social security and medicare; medicaid; federal, state, and local income taxes paid or to be paid to federal, state, and local governments is 31%, then by knowing this percentage, you can better determine how you will allocate (distribute) your money in the Cost of Living Budget.

Entrance Exams - The entrance exam is a test or exam a student is required to take in order to be considered for admission to a college or university. The student must earn a minimum test score to be considered. For a Bachelor's degree, a student is usually required to take an SAT or ACT exam. For a Master's degree, a student is usually required to take the GMAT for business or GRE for most other degrees and sometimes business, depending on the college or university. For a PhD, a student is usually required to take the GRE.

Excel – Excel is a software program, owned and licensed by the Microsoft Corporation, used to build spreadsheets, tables, and graphs. A spreadsheet is very useful for analyzing numbers and can be used to generate tables and graphs for further analysis.

FDIC (Federal Deposit Insurance Corporation) – The FDIC is a government entity and regulates the financial services industry. Currently, FDIC also provides federal deposit insurance up to $250,000 per person per financial institution. However, this can change, and you should refer to www.fdic.gov for more information.

FICA (Federal Insurance Contributions Act) – is the combination of social security taxes and Medicare taxes we pay. Social Security and Medicare taxes usually show up as FICA taxes on your paycheck.

Federal Housing Administration (FHA) – FHA is a federal government entity. FHA has set guidelines on how much borrowers can afford to borrow. FHA provides mortgage insurance to FHA approved lending institutions.

Field – A field is a type/discipline of work such as Accounting, Medicine, Astronomy, Psychology, Mechanical Engineering, and Genetic Research. A field is more job specific than an Industry. See Industry.

Goal – A goal is an end result that you *plan* to achieve. Sometimes the terms *goal* and *objective* are used interchangeably.

Gross Income – Gross income is your income before paying any taxes. If your only income was your salary (and you did not have a bank account earning interest), then your salary would be your gross income. If you earned $40,000 in salary for one year's worth of work and you had no other income such as from interest earned in a savings account, then your gross income would be $40,000 for the year.

Definitions (Cont'd)

Home Equity Loan – A home equity loan allows you to borrow the amount of equity you have in your home. Equity is the current value of your home minus the balance you owe on your home. For example, if your home is valued at $100,000 and the outstanding balance you owe on your home is $80,000, you have $20,000 in equity. If you fail to make your loan payments, you could lose your home, because your home is used as collateral when taking out a home equity loan. Some states have outlawed home equity loans.

IRS or Internal Revenue Service – The IRS is responsible for obtaining revenue (money) for the federal government in order to operate the federal government for the benefit of the country as a whole. Revenue for the government is obtained through taxing individuals and businesses. Federal income taxes or personal income taxes at the federal level are filed with the IRS.

Ideal and Ultimate Job – The ideal and ultimate job is the job you really want to do after you graduate from college and have been working for say 10 or 20 years. The ideal and ultimate job is the job you plan to work toward on an identified career path. Your ideal and ultimate job may be your second job after you graduate from college or your sixth job after you graduate from college. It is totally up to you. Your ideal and ultimate job most likely will change over time as opportunities arise, circumstances change, skills develop, and interests evolve.

Income – Income is money that is earned.

Industry – An industry is a marketplace sector such as government, automotive, banking, healthcare, food, packaging, software, computers, oil and gas, wind energy, and agriculture. A field is more job specific than an industry. See Field.

Interest Rate, Adjustable – Adjustable or variable interest rate loans have *changing* interest rates that are tied to a key financial indicator in the market, such as the prime rate, of which you have no control. You need to review the loan terms to understand how frequently the rate can change, by how much the rate can change, and how high the interest rate can be during the life of the loan (interest rate ceiling). See Table 11, Calculating Loan Payments. Compare to Fixed Interest Rate.

Interest Rate, Fixed – Fixed interest rate loans use the *same* interest rate throughout the life of the loan. See Table 11, Calculating Loan Payments. Compare to Adjustable Interest Rate.

Leadership - A leader is someone who inspires people and convinces them to follow him or her to achieve a positive goal. A leader Is one who possesses and demonstrates leadership skills. Leadership skills are behaviors, such as communicating positively and taking initiative, that are natural to the individual and also can be learned by anyone for whom leadership does not come naturally.

MBA or Master of Business Administration – The MBA is a two year degree in business, which can be pursued after completing a bachelor's degree.

MD or Medical Doctor - An MD degree is typically pursued after completing a bachelor's degree. If you are interested in becoming a Medical Doctor, consider becoming a DO, an Osteopathic physician.

Master's Degree – A master's degree is usually a two year degree which is pursued after completing a bachelor's degree. A master's degree can be earned in almost any field.

Medicare - Medicare is a federal health insurance program for the elderly and for some disabled.

Money Market Account – A money market account is a type of savings account offered by financial institutions. Typically a money market account has higher interest rates than a traditional savings account. A Money Market Account at an FDIC insured bank is FDIC insured.

Money Market Fund – A money market fund is a type of mutual fund and is *not* FDIC insured.

Mortgage – A mortgage is a specific type of loan. A mortgage is a loan obtained from a financial institution to buy a home or other real estate and must be repaid. Compare to Loan.

PhD or Doctor of Philosophy – A PhD degree can be earned in almost any field and is typically pursued after completing a bachelor's degree and master's degree. A PhD is the highest level of education. Oftentimes PhD's go on to teach at colleges and universities, work as scientists, or serve in leadership roles in government, business, and not-for-profit organizations. A PhD is not to be confused with a MD (Medical Doctor).

Personal Lifetime Standard (PLS) – The PLS, from the Cost of Living Budget, is how much money you are willing to pay per month for "Housing" and "Non-housing" obligations based on a percentage of your gross income. The PLS should be lower than FHA's standard/formula.

Definitions (Cont'd)

Prime Rate – The prime rate is an interest rate set by the federal government. If the federal government wants to *increase* spending of goods and services in the overall economy, it lowers the interest rate, as a result, encourages borrowing. We are more likely to buy cars, homes, and expensive items if we are able to borrow money at a favorable interest rate. In addition, the Fed might lower the interest rate with the purpose to head-off a recession. During a recession, **GDP (Gross Domestic Product)**, the value of all goods (products) and services produced in the U.S. economy, declines over a period of time. To say it a different way, during a recession, people spend less money. If the federal government wants to *decrease* spending of goods and services in the overall economy, it increases the interest rate, and as a result, discourages borrowing. The federal government might increase the interest rate to head-off inflation. Lots of money in the marketplace tends to fuel inflation, high prices. Financial institutions use the published federal prime rate index to set their own interest rates at a margin so that they will make money. You will find many adjustable loan interest rates use the prime rate as its basis index. The federal government also sets the **discount rate**, the rate at which the government charges banks for borrowing money. The federal government controls the availability of money in the marketplace, **money supply**, by making adjustments to the prime rate and discount rate.

Principal – With respect to income, principal is the amount of money in a checking, savings, or money market account that is earning interest. With respect to loans, principal is the amount of money you owe the bank, excluding interest.

Progressive Tax System – A progressive tax system simply means, the more money you make, the higher your tax rate. The less money you make, the lower your tax rate. If you review the IRS's tax tables on the 1040 Instructions, you will see how it works, by looking at different income levels and taxes due on the tax tables and calculating tax rates or percentage of taxes due based on that information. To calculate the tax rate or percentage of taxes due, just for this exercise, divide the taxes due by income. The answer is the tax rate. (This is NOT the effective tax rate.)

Promotable Position – A promotable position is one in which a person serving in the position can be promoted to a management position within a company. Some company cultures separate management and administrative/technical/staff positions. If the position is classified as an administrative/technical/staff position, most likely the position will not be promotable to management. However, the only way to be sure is to ask before you accept the position. You should be sure to ask the hiring manager *and* to ask the Recruiter at the very least. If either one of them tells you "no" the position is not promotable, then the position most likely is not promotable.

Recruiter – A recruiter is someone who works either for an employer or an employment agency who seeks to hire (recruit) new employees.

Salary – Salary is what an employer offers to pay you for your work. Salary is expressed in monthly or annual terms. Some employers pay a salary plus a bonus for good work performed. Some employers will not pay a bonus if you have not performed well or if the company has not performed well; therefore you cannot count on receiving a bonus. You should not include any bonus potential when applying for loans.

Social Security - Social Security is a federal program that delivers income to those who are retired and to the disabled. Social Security is deducted from our paycheck today, and it immediately pays benefits to retirees and the disabled.

Socioeconomic Status – Using the term socioeconomic status is a method economists, psychologists, newspapers, governments, businesses, and others use to classify individuals and groups, with the purpose to understand their customers in the case of a business, understand why an event occurred, or prevent an event from occurring in the future. The socioeconomic status of a group of persons in a study may consider sex, age, race, national origin, income level, education level, or geography, among others. You will notice during a Presidential election, analysts talk a lot about the socioeconomic status of a candidate's voters. If you read the References section at the end of this book, you will find tables from the U.S. Census Bureau, which include socioeconomic data. The terms socioeconomic data and demographic data are sometimes used interchangeably.

Values – Values are what is important to *you* when it comes to your work environment, work culture, and personal life.

Index

CPSIA information can be obtained at www.ICGtesting.com
Printed in the USA
LVOW03s1447270115

424564LV00001B/17/P